BUY THE FUTURE

LEARNING TO NEGOTIATE FOR A FUTURE BETTER THAN YOUR PRESENT

Buy The Future
Learning to Negotiate for a Future
Better than Your Present

Pneumalife Publishing
4423 Forbes Blvd
Lanham, MD 20706
www.pneumalife.com

Cover design by Synatse

Interior design by Kweku Ewusie-Mensah

ISBN 1-56229-190-4

DEDICATION

I dedicate this book to the memory of my mother – Dinah Otabil – who departed this life when I was still young; but imparted beneficial values to me, to last a life time. Ma, your life, though short, was worth it and I am eternally grateful to God for allowing you to nurture me.

TABLE OF CONTENTS

◈◈◈◈◈

Dedication... ii

Acknowledgements.. vii

Preface   – The Story...................................... ix

Chapter 1   – A Tale Of Two Paradigms.............. 1

Chapter 2   – The Field Man And The Tent Man.. 17

Chapter 3   – Who Is Stronger? 35

Chapter 4   – The Hungry Hunter...................... 51

Chapter 5   – Jacob Negotiates With His

                        Prepared Stew............................. 69

Chapter 6   – Do You Understand What You

                        Just Signed?............................... 93

Chapter 7   – The Real Cost Of Jacob's Stew 103

Chapter 8   – Don't Go Too Far For Your Goats... 111

Chapter 9   – The Blessing Of The Birthright..... 131

Chapter 10 – Esaus With Bad Attitude.............. 143

Chapter 11 – When Esaus Become Jacobs.......... 153

ACKNOWLEDGEMENTS

I am extremely indebted to the twins - Esau and Jacob - whose lives, as recorded in the Bible, inspired the concepts for this book. Their values and choices continue to instruct me in negotiating the various phases of my life.

In writing this book, I benefited immensely from the comments of my good friend - Charles Awasu - an economics professor, who critiqued my initial thoughts as if I was sitting for a test in one of his classes!

I also benefited from the perspectives of Denise Anatsui, Cephas Narh and Mina Akita who gave me audience comments on the book. Mr. Isaac Obeng and Anna Ewusie-Mensah helped with the copy editing of the manuscript.

I remain indebted to all those who heard me express these concepts, when I first shared them in my sermons and urged me to turn them into a book.

Most of all, to my partner and wife - Joy - who became my sounding board throughout the period of writing. And to my children - Sompa, Nhyira, Yoofi and Baaba - whose future and destiny continue to challenge me to think.

Preface

THE STORY

◇◇◇◇◇

The thesis of this book is based on the principles gleaned from this Biblical story of the lives of Esau and Jacob.

Isaac was forty years old when he took Rebekah as wife, the daughter of Bethuel the Syrian of Padan Aram, the sister of Laban the Syrian. Now Isaac pleaded with the LORD for his wife, because she was barren; and the LORD granted his plea, and Rebekah his wife conceived. But the children struggled together within her; and she said, "If all is well, why am I like this?" So she went to inquire of the LORD. And the LORD said to her:

"Two nations are in your womb, Two peoples shall be separated from your body; One people shall be stronger than the other, And the older shall serve the younger."

So when her days were fulfilled for her to give birth, indeed there were twins in her womb. And the first came out red. He was like a hairy garment all over; so they called his name Esau. Afterward his brother came out, and his hand took hold of Esau's heel; so his name was called Jacob. Isaac was sixty years old when she bore them.

So the boys grew. And Esau was a skillful hunter, a man of the field; but Jacob was a mild man, dwelling in tents. And Isaac loved Esau because he ate of his game, but Rebekah loved Jacob.

Now Jacob cooked a stew; and Esau came in from the field, and he was weary. And Esau said to Jacob, "Please feed me with that same red stew, for I am weary." Therefore his name was called Edom. But Jacob said, "Sell me your birthright as of this day." And Esau said, "Look, I am about to die; so what is this birthright to me?" Then Jacob said, "Swear to me as of this day." So he swore to him, and sold his birthright to Jacob. And Jacob gave Esau bread and stew of lentils; then he ate and drank, arose, and went his way. Thus Esau despised his birthright.

Now it came to pass, when Isaac was old and his eyes were so dim that he could not see, that he called Esau his older son and said to him, "My son." And he answered him, "Here I am." Then he said, "Behold now, I am old. I do not know the day of my death. Now therefore, please take your weapons, your quiver and your bow, and go out to the field and hunt game for me. And make me savory food, such as I love, and bring it to me that I may eat, that my soul may bless you before I die."

Now Rebekah was listening when Isaac spoke to Esau his son. And Esau went to the field to hunt game and to bring it. So Rebekah spoke to Jacob her son, saying, "Indeed I heard your father speak to Esau your brother, saying, 'Bring me game and make savory food for me, that I may eat it and bless you in the presence of the LORD before my death.' "Now therefore, my son, obey my voice according to what I command you. Go now to the flock and bring me from there two choice kids of the goats, and I will make savory food from them for your father, such as he loves. Then you shall take it to your father, that he may eat it, and that he may bless you before his death." And Jacob said to Rebekah his mother, "Look, Esau my brother is a hairy man, and I am a smooth-skinned man. Perhaps my father will feel me, and I shall seem to be a deceiver to him; and I shall bring a curse on myself and not a blessing." But his mother said to him, "Let your curse be on me, my son; only obey my voice, and go, get them for me." And he went and got them and brought them to his mother, and his mother made savory food, such as his father loved. Then Rebekah took the choice clothes of her elder son Esau, which were with her in the house, and put them on Jacob her younger son. And she put the skins of the kids of the goats on his hands and on the smooth part of his neck. Then she gave the savory food and the bread, which she had prepared, into the hand of her son Jacob.

So he went to his father and said, "My father.' And he said, "Here I am. Who are you, my son?" Jacob said to his father, "I am Esau your firstborn; I have done just as you told me; please arise, sit and eat of my game, that your soul may bless me." But Isaac said to his son, "How is it that you have found it so quickly, my son?" And he said, "Because the LORD your God brought it to me." Then Isaac said to Jacob, "Please come near, that I may feel you, my son, whether you are really my son Esau or not." So Jacob went near to Isaac his father, and he felt him and said, "The voice is Jacob's voice, but the hands are the hands of Esau." And he did not recognize him, because his hands were hairy like his brother Esau's hands; so he blessed him. Then he said, "Are you really my son Esau?" He said, "I am." He said, "Bring it near to me, and I will eat of my son's game, so that my soul may bless you." So he brought it near to him, and he ate; and he brought him wine, and he drank. Then his father Isaac said to him, "Come near now and kiss me, my son." And he came near and kissed him; and he smelled the smell of his clothing, and blessed him and said:

"Surely, the smell of my son Is like the smell of a field Which the LORD has blessed. Therefore may God give you Of the dew of heaven, the fatness of the earth, And plenty of grain and wine. Let peoples serve you, And nations bow down to you. Be master over your brethren, And let your mother's sons bow down to you. Cursed be everyone who curses you, And blessed be those who bless you!"

Now it happened, as soon as Isaac had finished blessing Jacob, and Jacob had scarcely gone out from the presence of Isaac his father, that Esau his brother came in from his hunting. He also had made savory food, and brought it to his father, and said to his father, "Let my father arise and eat of his son's game, that your soul may bless me." And his father Isaac said to him, "Who are you?" So he said, "I am your son, your firstborn, Esau." Then Isaac trembled exceedingly, and said, "Who? Where is the one who hunted game and brought it to me? I ate all of it before you came, and I have blessed him--and indeed he shall be blessed."

When Esau heard the words of his father, he cried with an exceedingly great and bitter cry, and said to his father, "Bless me--me also, O my father!" But he said, "Your brother came with deceit and has taken away your blessing." And Esau said, "Is he not rightly named Jacob? For he has supplanted me these two times. He took away my birthright, and now look, he has taken away my blessing!" And he said, "Have you not reserved a blessing for me?" Then Isaac answered and said to Esau, "Indeed I have made him your master, and all his brethren I have given to him as servants; with grain and wine I have sustained him. What shall I do now for you, my son?" And Esau said to his father, "Have you only one blessing, my father? Bless me--me also, O my father!" And Esau lifted up his voice and wept.

Then Isaac his father answered and said to him:

"Behold, your dwelling shall be of the fatness of the earth, And of the dew of heaven from above. By your sword you shall live ,And you shall serve your brother; And it shall come to pass, When you become restless, That you shall break his yoke from your neck."

So Esau hated Jacob because of the blessing with which his father blessed him, and Esau said in his heart, "The days of mourning for my father are at hand; then I will kill my brother Jacob." And the words of Esau her older son were told to Rebekah. So she sent and called Jacob her younger son, and said to him, "Surely your brother Esau comforts himself concerning you by intending to kill you. Now therefore, my son, obey my voice: arise, flee to my brother Laban in Haran. And stay with him a few days, *until your brother's fury turns away, until your brother's anger turns away from you, and he forgets what you have done to him; then I will send and bring you from there. Why should I be bereaved also of you both in one day?"* **Genesis 25:20-34; 27:1-45 NKJV**

Chapter 1

A TALE OF TWO PARADIGMS

Two nations are in your womb,
Two peoples shall be separated from your body;

The story of Esau and Jacob shows us how individuals who started life together, end up growing in different ways, develop different value systems and make different choices about their destinies.

Not long ago, I had lunch with an old schoolmate of mine from primary school. We were very good pals in the early years of our lives growing up in Ghana's port city of Tema but we had lost touch with each other for so many years as we pursued different vocations in life. He had turned into a brilliant and successful legal scholar and I had become a reverend minister and an educator. As children of average working class parents, we were both very proud of each other's achievements and went down memory lane to reminiscence on years gone by and friends long forgotten. As we tried to piece up the little information we could put together on who was where and what some of our classmates were doing, we were amazed at how life had turned out for most of us after thirty years. Some had turned out very well in their chosen fields, but the stations which others occupied made it very difficult to reconcile with the fact that, we all began together, played the same games, sat under the same teachers and shared similar dreams of future significance.

The stories of a couple of our mates were very heartbreaking. Some who had started out with a lot of promise had ended up in very distressing and depressing circumstances. Their present situations did not in any way reflect the promise of their earlier performance in the classroom. How could a sharp, talented and top-of-the-class student end up in a job as a casual field worker on a farm? How could a young man with great leadership skills settle for a job as a third rate wayside carpenter? How does a beautiful, non-promiscuous, decent, intelligent, and bright girl manage to have three children out of wedlock before she is twenty years and later have a busload of kids from different men without any thriving source of livelihood? On and on, we recounted story after story. Stories of people we had sat in class with and shared so much of our life with.

WHAT WENT WRONG?

I was quiet for a while as I pondered the whole concept of life and what we make of it. I asked my friend, 'what went wrong - at what point in our lives did we start drifting into different directions?' It was a question that had engaged my thinking and prayerful consideration for the last several years. My friend simply replied, 'I don't know'. As we continued eating, I kept thinking, 'Why does our future often so contradict our present? Is there a way in which we can determine our future today? Are there some things we do that make us prone to success and others we do that make us prone to failure? Can we determine the outcome of our future today?' These are questions that I suppose all of us have given some thought to. Our elders in Africa have a saying that '*you can determine the output of a crop from its germination*'. There is some truth to that but I have seen people who 'germinated' very beautifully but failed to produce a good crop. I have seen very 'good' boys who became crooks later in life as well as 'bad' boys who managed to pull their lives out of destruction into a better life. I have seen organizations and nations outdoored with great fanfare and promise, but failed to deliver on their promise.

Two people can be born under very similar circumstances go through similar experiences and yet arrive at different destinies. People sit in the same classroom and listen to the same teacher, use the same textbooks, do the same assignments, sometimes even get the same grades, but then as they grow into their future roles, they do not achieve the same levels of success in their individual pursuits. The same applies to corporate bodies, organizations and nations.

Most of us have had that bitter-sweet reunion with

an old neighbourhood or school acquaintance after about ten, fifteen or thirty years of separation and realized that although the two of you have a lot to talk about in the past, you have very little in common to share with your present lives. Sometimes you become aware rather painfully, that whilst you might have made a lot of meaningful progress with your life, your friend is still basically settled at the same place he was when you last parted company. Your conversation after a few nostalgic jokes and back slapping, lapses into an awkward silence. Your beginning was similar but your present has become very different. Sometimes it would not be your friend who is lagging behind but you becoming aware of your own personal underdevelopment. You realize that whilst your friend has made some impressive hop-step-jump, you are still warming up on the fringes of the tracks of life.

Even identical twins who were developed out of the same fertilized human egg, grew in the same womb, got nurtured by the same parents and shared clothing, friends and educational experiences in their formative years do not always end up in their adult life with the same levels of performance and achievement. One may become more successful with their chosen profession or career whilst the other never manages to find happiness and success with their lives.

Part of the reason for the way people turn out differently has to do with two vital factors:

1. The values they develop for their lives

2. The way they see life and respond to it

These two vital factors ultimately, shape all the important decisions people make. When we are children, we receive our values and perspectives from our parents and the larger community we leave in. As we grow up, we use our powers of self-awareness, imagination and choice to either affirm what we learnt at home or create a new set of values and perspectives. For some of my childhood friends, their future was marred by the wrong values of their parents and the decisions they made on their behalf. Others probably responded to the wrong values they saw in their community and just implemented them in their lives.

> As we grow up we use our powers of self-awareness, imagination and choice to either affirm what we learnt at home or create a new set of values and perspectives.

IS IT FATE OR CHOICE?

Some observe the various outcomes of life and conclude that it is all a matter of fate and destiny. That man has no control over what the final outcome will be. That is a very sad way to look at life. To think that God created man to just go through life like a robot preprogrammed without options, simply to act in certain predetermined ways, is biblically flawed. One of the first responsibilities of man in the garden of Eden was to exercise his power of choice and to live in the consequences of his choice. The choice to either eat of the tree that gives us life or the one that produces death was the prerogative of man. If God has given us the power of choice then it means the quality of our choices impact directly on the quality of our lives. The basis we use in formulating our choices, therefore becomes crucial to the quality of choices we make and the resulting quality of life we lead. They will determine:

- Whether we live in the comfort of what we have today or create better opportunities for tomorrow

- Whether we live on what we have today or save to invest for tomorrow

- Whether our choices fulfill short term needs or long term purposes

- Whether we allow the desperation of today to make us ignore the consequences of our decisions on our future

There are those who work with a value system that is focused on short-term needs and tend to make decisions that seem beneficial today but become disastrous in the future. I call such people and nations, Esaus. On the other hand there are those who work with a value system that is focused on long-term benefits instead of short-term needs. They save what they have today and invest it for greater benefit in the future. I call them, Jacobs.

ESAU AND JACOB

The biblical narrative of the lives of Jacob and Esau illustrates how our values, beliefs and assumptions in life shape our destinies differently. It provides us with an insight into how different personal and corporate cultures develop their skills, make choices and manage their God-given resources.

Before Jacob and Esau were born, their parents, Isaac and Rebecca had prayed to God for a miracle of birth after twenty years of no children in their marriage. God heard their prayer and granted their desire. Rebecca became pregnant. This was a pregnancy that was special because of the prayer of faith of Isaac and Rebecca. In the process of time, Rebecca started feeling very uncomfortable because of the boisterous movements in her womb. She sensed a struggle within her. The situation got so bad that they had to go back to God for explanation.

The Lord confirmed their joy that not only was Rebecca pregnant; she was actually carrying a set of twins in her womb. Now, that is what we call a double portion. God goes ahead to tell them that although these two people are twins and come from the same womb their destinies would be different.

"Two nations are in your womb,
Two peoples shall be separated from your body;

NATIONS AND PEOPLES

Although Rebecca was pregnant with twins who were

just two individuals, God called them, 'nations' and 'peoples'. The children in the womb were prophetic pictures of the characteristics of nations and peoples. There would be nations who would be modeled after the value systems of these children. There would also be people who would model their lives and choices after the characteristics of these twins. Because God knows the end from the beginning, He gave Isaac and Rebecca a picture of their children's future. He did not pre-program their choices in the future. All God did was to tell the parents through fore-knowledge, how the twins were going to turn out.

Both twins were conceived and born as a direct result of God's answer to Isaac's prayer. None of the two children came from the devil. Both of them came from God. When they were born, the first twin was called Esau and the second, Jacob. Following the reference of God to them as *Nations* and People, we would say that the birth of Esau and Jacob represented the birth of Nations and Peoples. The later choices of Esau and Jacob also represent the kind of choices Nations and People continue to make as well as the implications and consequences of their choices.

It is important to note right away that, when we speak of Esau and Jacob, we are not limited to the two particular individuals involved in this drama. Esau and Jacob have a wider trans-generational and transcultural reference. They represent humanity and how we conduct our affairs as both nations and individuals.

- There are *Esau Nations* and there are *Jacob Nations*.

- There are *Esau People* and there are *Jacob People*.

Esau and Jacob represent two different ways for achieving personal or organizational development. They show us how the form of our values, beliefs and assumptions, shape the way we relate to other people and also make decisions. The form and shape of our values and beliefs is known as our paradigm.

PARADIGMS AND MOULDS

Think of a paradigm as a manufacturer's mould into which he pours the fluid substances he wants to shape into a solid form. A member of my congregation who owns and runs a plastic factory, took me round his factory to see how plastic products like cups and plates are made. I did not understand all the technical processes but I got to know that they had to first carve a mould into which they pour in the liquid plastic. If the mould is that of a cup, it produces cups; if it is a plate it produces plates. I realized that the shape of the mould determined the shape that is produced. Through this procedure, thousands of cups are produced by one mould. Just as one mould produces several thousands of cups, so one paradigm can produce so many people who think in the way that paradigm has shaped them.

Consider what will happen to all the cups produced from a faulty mould? If the moulds are faulty, the products will also become faulty. In the same way when a person or nation operates with a faulty paradigm, that person or nation will come out faulty. Their lives will take on the shape of the paradigm that produced them. When God said to Rebecca, 'Two nations are in your womb, Two peoples shall be separated from your body,' He was using the value and belief systems which would later be operated by these twins, to establish a very important basis for understanding the value and belief systems of nations and people.

> If the moulds are faulty, the products will also become faulty. In the same way when a person or nation operates with a faulty paradigm, that person or nation will come out faulty.

SPECTACLES AND CARS

A paradigm is also like the pair of spectacles through which we view ourselves and our world. When you put on a rose-coloured pair of spectacles, everything you see will appear rose-coloured. Even those of different colour will be re-coloured by the colour of your spectacles. A paradigm determines the way you see things. It also determines what you see and do not see. I learnt this lesson many years ago when I had my first car. It was a tiny little red coloured Fiat. I loved that car so much although it gave me so many problems. By the time it got to me it was an over-aged vehicle that had already lived out the best part of its life and was now just surviving on grace. As a result of its old age it had become quiet grumpy and had a mind of its own. That Fiat could just decide not to move right in the middle of heavy traffic to simply attract attention to itself and huge embarrassment for me. With a lot of coaxing and pushing, it would reluctantly get back on the road and sputter for the rest of the journey. Many times, it simply refused to come home with me by deciding to spend the night or a few days out in the mechanic's workshop, to hang out with other disgruntled fiats. In spite of all its grumpiness, I still loved that little red Fiat. It was my first car and my first love.

THE POWER OF RECOGNITION

Something happened to my power of recognition when it first entered my life. Whereas I had never been keen with Fiats prior to owning one, I all of a sudden began to notice all the Fiats of my make in town. I could spot a Fiat way out there in the traffic. My powers of recognition for Fiats were activated. I took notice of them when they drove past me in traffic and developed an interest in guessing how old they were and whether they looked better than mine. I formed a mental fraternity with all owners of my make of Fiat and exchanged a knowing smile with them when we met in traffic. Especially if the colour of the car was red like mine,

I just felt like the owner was a real comrade. As a matter of fact I knew the license plate numbers of the other owners of red Fiat I met frequently on the road.

Because of my car's frequent mechanical shut-downs, I got to know of every Fiat mechanic in town. I knew about the engineering of a Fiat and what its weaknesses and strengths were. I knew where to get the best Fiat parts also. All these I did simply because I owned and used a Fiat. That Fiat had became the reference point from which I viewed and evaluated my vehicular world. When it entered my life it shaped my vehicular paradigm and opened my eyes to the world of Fiats which existed but never caught my attention. It shaped what I noticed and did not notice. It shaped my alliances and networks. It shaped my interests and knowledge acquisition. That is what a paradigm does. It is like wearing a coloured spectacle which colours your view of the world and how you respond to it.

The next car I had was a Volkswagen Golf. When I got it I went through the same process as the Fiat. I never knew there were so many *Golfs* in town until I owned one. With all the cars I have owned, I go through the same process as I did with my first beloved Fiat, only with less intensity. Through the experience with my Fiat, I learnt that where you sit and what you sit in determines what you see. The levels of productivity that individuals and organizations can attain to, are directly related to what they perceive as the way to attain success. If you sit with Esau, you will see success from Esau's perspective. If you sit with Jacob, you will see success from Jacob's perspective. People see life from where they are. If, for some reason, you sit in the seat of scarcity, you will only see scarcity even if your environment abounds in wealth. If you sit in the seat of mockers and the scornful, you will depreciate the value of all that God has given to you. If you sit in the seat of the righteous, you will honour what God gives to you.

> People see life from where they are. If, for some reason, you sit in the seat of scarcity, you will only see scarcity even if your environment abounds in wealth.

YOUR VALUES SHAPE YOUR ATTRACTIONS AND INTERESTS

There are people who remember every goal scored by their favourite soccer team in the last twenty years but cannot remember anything from their history class. Others notice every little detail in the make of their music stereo system but cannot see the details in their financial statement. Some can understand the logic in rap music yet they cannot unravel the true causes of their poverty and under-achievement. All these people sit in different seats and see different things. What engages their attention and seriousness is shaped by what they see as important. There are those who pick the morning newspaper and turn first to the sports page; others turn first to the financial page. You can't make the sports page your priority and master your finances at the same time; neither can you turn first to the financial page and master your knowledge in sports. You gain mastery in the area that engages your priority.

Nations build their developmental paradigm after their national values; those values will make them either an *Esau Nation* or they are a *Jacob Nation*. Nations with an Esau paradigm solve their problems in a very different manner from nations with a Jacob paradigm. Individuals also view their lives from either an Esau or a Jacob paradigm and solve their problems within the limits of that paradigm. Poor nations are poor because of their productivity values and rich nations are rich because of their productivity values. Values ultimately dictate policy and priority.

> Values ultimately dictate policy and priority.

THE STRUGGLE

As babies growing in the womb of Rebecca, Esau and Jacob created an internal struggle within her. God used that struggle to dramatise the antagonism of the two different world views growing within her. That struggle still continues. It is a struggle between the Esau way and the Jacob way. In personal relationships, in the corporate world, in community development, in international relations, this struggle continues to be waged. Much of the discomfort we feel in our world is founded on how these two different paradigms manage both their personal resources and the society's.

The thrust of this book is to help you identify which

side of the struggle you are on and to observe how these two paradigms influenced the priorities and choices of Esau and Jacob and continue to exert their influence over people and nations in our time. Much as the practical realities of the world of Esau and Jacob differ vastly from what our generation has to deal with, the under-girding assumptions that shape our choices are all the same as what shaped theirs. The two moulds are the same then as they are today, but the contents that we pour into those moulds may be different. As we track the growth and progress of these twins, you will be able to locate yourself, family, company, community or nation within the behavioral patterns of Esau and Jacob. You will understand why you are where you are in your life. You will understand why your family is where it is and why your community or nation has the problems it has. You will identify the philosophies that guide your life and the implications of those philosophies to your future. The future is either bought or sold by the choices of today; and the choices of today are influenced by the paradigm you operate from.

> The future is either bought or sold by the choices of today; and the choices of today are influenced by the paradigm you operate from.

■ The main feature of the Esau paradigm is that it sacrifices the opportunities and potential of the future in order to fulfill the necessities of the present. Esau sells the future to buy the present. He also responds to his challenges through the application of old traditional methods.

■ The main feature of the Jacob paradigm is that it harnesses the resources of the present in order to acquire the opportunities and potential of the future. Jacob sells the present to buy the future. He responds to his challenges through the application of innovation.

These key features of the Esau/Jacob value system influenced the habits they formed and the point of view they brought to bear on their choices. Understanding the Esau and Jacob paradigms will help you to locate the center of your own values and how you deploy your gifts and talents to achieve your life goals. The challenge today is not just to discover and use your gifts and talents, but to use them in such a way that you don't end up disadvantaged in your negotiations with life. You will discover from this book that you cannot operate from an Esau paradigm and expect the blessings related to the Jacob paradigm.

Chapter 2

THE FIELD MAN
AND THE TENT MAN

◇◇◇◇◇

*So the boys grew. And Esau was a skillful hunter, a
man of the field; but Jacob was a mild man,
dwelling in tents.*

We are responsible for our choices. The fundamental basis for any judgment of our actions
is based on the principle of personal responsibility. The reason God judges us is because He gave us
the power to choose. All of us were born into a world
where choices had already been made by people who had
lived before us. Those choices produced consequences
which we inherited, but within that situation, God also
gave us the power of conscience and self-awareness to
enable us judge the rightness and wrongness of the different values and cultural options available to us. As we

grow in life the choices we make define us.

The biblical narrative does not say much about the influences that shaped the values and beliefs of Esau and Jacob except the fact that Isaac had a liking for Esau whilst Rebecca favoured Jacob. As young boys growing within their society, there may have been so many influences from parents and their community for them to choose from. It may be deduced that, Esau was influenced more by his father, whilst Jacob was influenced by his mother. The extent of that influence on their character and value formation cannot be fully verified. However, as human beings, they were not just there to reflect any and every norm from their parents and society. They also had the power to choose their responses to what was happening around them.

GROWTH AMPLIFIES CHARACTER

It is just amazing what growth can produce in people. *So the boys grew. And Esau was a skillful hunter, a man of the field; but Jacob was a mild man, dwelling in tents.* When we are little, we all look very much alike. Babies look alike - they are all cute, sweet, adorable and promising. We are all enamoured with babies. We sing to them, coo to them and make funny faces at them all because they look so innocent and pure. We see all of them as destined for greatness. Then growth comes in and reveals all their hidden flaws. Growth is like a microscope. When it is focused on seemingly orderly and fine objects, we discover images that contradict the first impressive images of what we saw.

Every drunk on the sidewalk used to be a beautiful baby with promise. The prisons are full of people who used to be sweet little bundles of joy to older people. The violent gang leader used to be a nice smiling and happy little child. So what happened to them? Well, let me tell you what happened. They grew up. Growth revealed the children's own sinfulness as well as the values and lessons imparted to them by the society they learnt from. Growth amplified the little character flaws we all took for granted. When flaws are not dealt with early in life, they become life long habits that work to our disadvantage as we grow. In the parable of the wheat and tares, Jesus Christ illustrated this principle that although the wheat and tares looked alike in the beginning, growth would reveal their true fruits. Fruits reveal true nature.

> Growth is like a microscope. When it is focused on seemingly orderly and fine objects, we discover images that contradict the first impressive images of what we saw.

ESAU AND JACOB GROW IN DIFFERENT DIRECTIONS

As young children, Esau and Jacob might have looked as any normal child in their community, but as they grew up, they chose different paths for their lives.

■ Esau is a skillful hunter and a man of the field.

■ Jacob is a mild man dwelling in tents.

These descriptions are almost opposite to the other. Although both children were answers to prayer, came from the same parents and grew up in the same environment, they chose different philosophies of life. They positioned themselves differently based on their understanding and philosophy of life. Remember that your actions are a playback of the philosophies that regulate your life.

ESAU THE SKILLFUL HUNTER

Esau grew up and set himself to work as a hunter. He hunted for game in the wild and survived economically from the benefits of his profession. But beyond the economic value he derived from his chosen profession, he built his lifestyle and choices around the values of his profession. As a matter of fact, people choose their professions because of who they are and how they function. We settle for professions that are suited to our personalities. This is not an absolute rule but a fair guide to how people make choices.

> People choose their professions because of who they are and how they function. We settle for professions that are suited to our personalities.

In the case of Esau and Jacob, their professions had a

lot to tell about their personalities. A hunter in the wild has a perspective of life that is different from a tent dweller. Esau was a hunter and dwelt in the wild. And he was good at his job. He is described in the scriptures as a skillful hunter.

As a hunter, Esau must have mastered these four very important skills.

Locate prey. Hunters are predators. A good hunter studies the movement of his prey. He spends time to make meaning out of the hoof prints of the animals he tracks. In the Kalahari Desert of South West Africa, there still exit people who can read the tracks of animals in the wild even weeks after the first imprints were made. They can determine the gender of the animal, its speed of movement and its intended location by making meaning out of a few hoof prints. They know where to find what they are looking for. Through training and tradition, hunters survive in the wild against the harsh terrains they operate in by tracking their prey.

Pursue. The hunter must be a good runner. He or she must have the physical build and stamina that enables them to run after what they are looking for. Hunters know how to stalk their prey until they are able to strike. In pursuing their prey, they run for very long distances and for several uncertain number of days with very little food. Hunters have a dogged determination when they are on a trail. They are silent in movement and quick on the feet.

Kill. Pursuit of the animal is expected to culminate in a kill for the hunter. He survives on what he kills. It is the life of the animal for his life. The hunter knows when to strike. He strikes with a lot of skill and power. Since experience has taught the hunter that a first miss may make all his effort meaningless, he makes sure to aim well and strike decisively.

Gather. The hunter knows how to bring in what he has caught or killed. After all the long periods of locating, pursuing and killing the prey, the hunter must bring his trophy home. He must have food for himself and his family, so he learns how to carry what he has gained in the field to his home.

These are very important skills that make the hunter prevail over his prey. However, the hunter has some limitations.

Hunters go for one animal at a time. The general operation of a hunter limits him to the pursuit of one target at a time. The hunter is single-minded in targeting his prey. He isolates his prey from the larger group in order to track it down. This is both a strength and a weakness. On one hand, it helps the hunter to focus his skills and energies on the pursuit and capture of his target. On the other hand, it limits the hunter to a slow process of tracking one prey at a time whilst his competitor devises more versatile means of capturing multiples of prey. It also limits the capacity of the hunter to the achievement of very limited task. Great skills and abilities are deployed to achieve very little results.

Resources that could have been used to achieve a lot, are used to achieve very little. Nations and people who manifest this tendency, spend enormous national and personal resources focusing on largely insignificant and unbeneficial objectives. It is like using a baseball bat to kill an ant. That baseball bat could do far more than just killing one ant. It could hit a homerun.

Hunters do not rear and husband the animals they need. Hunters do not build farms where they cultivate what they hunt for. In a sense, creating farms and husbanding what the hunter needs, takes the thrill out of his job and redefines his job. The thrill of hunting is found in the chase or the pursuit. Even if the target does not merit the energy expended, the hunting activity can still release a lot of adrenalin in the hunter. The down-side of adrenalin release is that, it overrides your power of reasoning and analysis. It can drive you to pursue targets without taking time to think about the benefits and long-term effects of what you are pursuing.

> The down-side of adrenaline release is that it overrides your power of reasoning and analysis. It can drive you to pursue targets without taking time to think about the benefits and long-term effects of what you are pursuing.

ACTIVITY IS NOT THE SAME AS PRODUCTIVITY

Many people run their lives on adrenalin and not wisdom and understanding. For such people, the pursuit of targets and the thrill derived from it become the end instead of the means to the end. They are excited by the activities they are involved in. For them, the chase is more fulfilling than the catch. Such are the ones who equate activity to productivity. There are people who are always excited about one new idea or the other. Today, they have a fantastic idea that would generate millions of dollars; the next day they have made the most significant contact with a very influential person that will lead to a major deal. They seem full of very juicy ideas and concepts to get something done. The only problem is that none of their many chases yield any catch. They seem to run on the high of their own pursuits. The maxim of such people seems to be, 'I am happy because I am hunting even if I never make a catch'. Because of the thrill derived from hunting, such hunters do not make any effort to husband and cultivate what they catch.

Generally speaking, most hunters work with the belief that their resources will always be available. They do not grasp the concept of times and seasons; that there are seasons of abundance and seasons of scarcity. They do not consider that those who survive and thrive in the season of scarcity are those who manage to stretch the benefits of their resources beyond its present abundance. It is possible to use the management principles of storage and preservation to enable you to continue enjoying what you have beyond the season of abundance. No human being has the genetic coding to allow them to be young and strong all their life, but good planning can make you enjoy the fruits of your strength when you are old and weak.

We have all read stories of people who were rich and famous but later became poor and destitute. Many athletes, entertainers and entrepreneurs have experienced the pain of falling from the top to the bottom. Even in the Christian ministry, I have encountered people who rose to the top and later tumbled in very sad circumstances.

When people operate from an Esau paradigm, they have the hunter's mentality and presume that what they have today will always be available and can also be accessed in the same way as they knew it today. When we allow that thinking to shape our choices, we fail to plan and manage the lifecycle of our present achievements to cater for us in the future. We should always keep in mind that what we have today is not for the use of today. What we have today gives us the currency to purchase what will be tomorrow. Today's advantages must be used to buy tomorrow's opportunities.

> No human being has the genetic coding to allow them to be young and strong all their life but good planning can make you enjoy the fruits of your strength when you are old and weak.

Hunters go out everyday to hunt for new prey. Because the hunter has not mastered the art and science of nurturing what is needed, he and his family do not have food security. When the animals in the wild are depleted, the hunter and his family are exposed to starvation. Their survival requires that the forest must always have stock of animals for them. The hunter is a servant to the vagaries and capriciousness of the weather. They build their expectations around the belief that the favourable environment and the natural resources they have will always be available to them. Whilst hunters go out everyday to look for what they need, cultivators prepare for the day of scarcity and make provision for the emergencies of life.

There are still nations whose whole productive cycles are determined by the rainfall patterns of their countries. Such nations trust in the availability of natural resources at all needed times. When resources are depleted or new and more sophisticated processes are needed to access the resources, they find themselves disadvantaged.

Esau was a skillful hunter. He had spent time in perfecting his talents into very useful skills. He was very good at his job and had excellent skills acquired over the years through practice. If the world was only inhabited by hunters, he would have had a very successful and happy life. Unfortunately for him the world was not populated by people with his worldview and orientation. There were other people who had developed skills of management and productivity that were different from his. Those other people did not only hunt, but cultivated and harnessed what was hunted for. Esau's brother Jacob was of that group. He was a cultivator. *Jacob was a mild man, dwelling in tents.*

JACOB THE TENT MAN

The first description of Jacob in the scriptures was that

he was a dweller in tents. This description had to do with his profession. The most valuable skill of a tent man in the days of Esau and Jacob was to cultivate. They took time to nurture and cultivate their products in order to enhance its quality and also to increase the quantity. This nurturing skill set the tent man apart from the hunter in very fundamental ways. All of us know that it is easier to destroy than to bring back to life. In the long run the work of the tent man helps to renew the environment.

The tent man was also a pastoral person, who stayed in his tent long enough in a location to have the time and space to cultivate a good and profitable product. Tent people did not stay in one place to totally exhaust all the resource capacity of that space. They actually moved their activities in cycles from one location to the other as they cultivated. One season they work a particular space. Then they leave the land for it to rebuild its productive capacity as they move on to new locations they vacated a few seasons ago.

JACOB THE MILD MAN

The second description of Jacob was that he was a *mild man*. This description had reference to his character. What does 'mild man' mean? The word rendered as 'mild' in the New King James Version is derived from the Hebrew word, *'Tam'*. It carries the ideas of a quite, gentle and upright person. That may sound contradictory to what most people think of when considering the character of Jacob. Most people see him as a trickster and a fraud who exploited his brother Esau. Jacob must be judged on the account of his character and not the meaning of his name. His name, 'Jacob' means 'supplanter' but the character reference from the Bible concerning him was 'an upright man'. His personal character did not reflect the meaning of his name. The manifestation of our character and the credible character references who vouch for us are more reliable than the names our parents choose to give us. In this case, the person called 'supplanter' ended up being described as an upright man. Jacob did not spend his time scheming to take advantage of people. He was not a callous self-serving opportunist. He developed a character that was very different from his name; he was an upright man. Later on in life, after a season of struggle for divine blessing, God rightly changed the name of Jacob to reflect his true heritage. The name he received from God was, Israel - meaning, 'a prince who prevails'.

Uprightness does not imply that he never sinned but that he did what was right at the right time and in the right way that did not violate the principles of God. Jacob stayed on the right side of God's principles. As we unveil his character more and more you will understand why there is misunderstanding concerning his choices and decisions in life.

'Mild man' also had reference to the character of Jacob as a quiet and contemplative person. He worked with his mind, developed ideas and used his creative mind to solve his problems. Further study of the life of Jacob reveals a man of enormous vision, imagination and innovation.

The main difference in the way Esau and Jacob approached life, was apparent in that phrase we looked at earlier, '*So the boys grew. And Esau was a skillful hunter, a man of the field; but Jacob was a mild man, dwelling in tents.*' **Genesis 25:27**

■ Esau as a hunter, operated from a productive paradigm that used much labour and physical energy to accomplish his tasks. He employed his great physical strength and athleticism as the main tool for his work.

■ Jacob as a quiet and contemplative cultivator, operated from the productive paradigm of using the power and force of imagination and calculated planning in accomplishing his tasks.

Jacob did not show much physical activity in his operations. The great activities that were playing out in Jacob's life occurred in his mind. The cogs and wheels running Jacob's life turned in his brains. Whilst Esau run with his feet after animals in the wild, Jacob run with his brains to discover a new and better way of husbanding and breeding the stock of animals he had.

> Whilst Esau run with his feet after animals in the wild, Jacob run with his brains to discover a new and better way of husbanding and breeding the stock of animals he had.

People who observed Jacob outwardly, probably thought he was doing nothing. Those people reasoned that if a person worked hard it must be observed through his physical activity and perspiration. In those people's world view, the harder people sweated, the more they were thought of as working hard. Jacob did not perspire much in the sun running after wild animals like his older brother Esau. He spent a lot of time, thinking about how to simplify the old procedures his society had inherited and functioned with.

■ Whilst Esau worked hard with the old systems he came to meet, Jacob worked hard in his mind to discover easier, faster and more efficient ways of doing what his society had been doing for years.

■ Through design and necessity, Jacob devised better ways of doing the tasks his community had undertaken over the years.

When he found the better way, it placed him in a position of great advantage over people who still held on to the old, slow and tired methods.

Jacob was a man of dreams, imagination and innovation. His brain was always ticking with new ideas and possibilities. Outwardly he looked calm and quiet but inwardly, swirling hurricanes of ideas were being processed into useful concepts. In that position of advantage in skills and strategy, he was able to negotiate better options for himself.

He did not manifest the athleticism and physical strength of his older brother and was probably seen by his father and the larger community as a slow starter who was uninvolved. The only one who believed in him was his mother. Jacob was 'momma's boy'. The father's preference was for Esau because he was a strong, athletic and capable hunter, who brought home all his special exotic meat from the wild. Isaac himself was a hard working farmer who had developed his economic wealth from the fortunes he inherited from his father Abraham. As a man used to physical hard work, he had a preference for his elder son Esau whose operations fitted more into the way he himself had functioned. Any time Esau went to hunt, he made sure to come home with what his father Isaac liked. Between the two of them there was a lot of understanding. They were all hard working field people.

THE HUNTER AND THE CULTIVATOR

The hunter is very different from the cultivator. The cultivator may not have much to begin with but will end up accumulating and deploying abundance of resources. The cultivator develops skills that help him to multiply the little he gets.

■ Those who breed and cultivate what they hunt for, are aware of the unreliability of the hunting expedition.

■ Cultivators major in the ability to harness their resources for use in a location that is easily assessable to them in times of need. They prepare to be ready for any opportunity that will knock on their door.

■ They patiently and systematically build up on their strengths and on the little they have. Cultivators create new wealth by wisely investing their old wealth. They embrace time as a friend and work patiently towards the future.

■ Instead of celebrating in abundance, they save up and take advantage of new investment opportunities that present themselves.

Jacob was a cultivator. He focused on nurturing and cultivating the little he had into abundance. He did not wait for abundance to happen by itself; he created abundance.

CHASERS AND NURTURERS

The culture of a hunter in the wild is based on the chase. The culture of the cultivator is based on the nurture. In life there are chasers and nurturers. When the hunter faces a competition, that demands the application of the principles of nurturing to achieve what is needed, the hunter stands sorely disadvantaged. The hunter will pursue one animal at a time and cannot even predict the quality and desirability of what he is pursuing. He could work so hard to find out later that what he has is not what he expected. The cultivator on the other hand, has the opportunity to choose from many options and be able to examine what he wants at close quarters in order to make the best choice. The cultivator does not take off blindly into the wild in hot and frenzied pursuit of a target he cannot be sure of. He has the advantage of careful examination to make his choices.

Between Esau and Jacob two different productive value systems emerged.

■ Esau's value system made him go out daily to hunt for what he needed. He followed in the routine of daily gathering what was enough.

■ The Jacob's value made him cultivate what would be needed. He followed the routine of nurturing and investing to increase the worth of what he had.

The big question is which of these systems was stronger? Is it the system that nurtures and increases value or the one that immediately uses all that is acquired?

Chapter 3

WHO IS STRONGER?

One people shall be stronger than the other

The first value judgment that God makes on the twins is that one will be stronger than the other. Remember that although the immediate recipients of that word were the twins in the womb of Rebecca, the larger import of what was declared had in mind the nations and peoples that patterned their lives after the moulds carved by the twins. The issue of the strength and resilience of the two value systems are important. determines our own personal preferences, for either of the systems that Esau and Jacob represented. I will assume in this book that, all of us desire to operate with and within a set of values and habits that gives us the skills to negotiate in life from a stronger vantage point.

COMPETITION AND PROGRESS

Human beings are competitive. We strive to surpass our previous performances and achievements. We also strive to surpass other people's performances and achievements. This urge to surpass previous performances is both natural and instinctive. We progress because of it. Some people and communities are very uncomfortable with the whole idea of competition. They prefer to see the world as a place of communalism where everyone strives very hard to stay at the same level with the others. When we perceive human development from that point of view, we stagnate our progress.

God is a God of diversity, creativity and growth. He evaluates and judges human performances and desires that our lives are not lived just to conform, but to transform. For a person to walk, he or she must put one foot ahead of the other and keep doing so till the destination is arrived at. It is natural to put one foot in front of the other. When we keep both feet in the same place there is no forward movement. Each one of us must develop the strength to put ourselves in a position to move forward and not just stay in a weakened position always. We can choose to operate from the system that makes us stronger and more effective in our life pursuits.

> For a person to walk, he or she must put one foot ahead of the other and keep doing so till the destination is arrived at. It is natural to put one foot in front of the other. When we keep both feet in the same place there is no forward movement.

THE CHALLENGE

The desire to get ahead makes all of us competitive. As human beings, we challenge ourselves to see what we are capable of doing and challenge others to find out whether we can do better than them. The question, 'who is stronger?' is asked daily.

When we were kids, we organized wrestling fights to find out who was stronger. We got bruises and cuts all over our bodies and later reprimands from our parents. I will never forget a particular girl in the neighbourhood. This girl was a very tough and accomplished fighter. She did not shy away from a good fight like the other girls. Since none of us boys wanted to earn the dubious reputation of having been beaten by a girl, we all stayed clear of her and pretended that she was too tomboyish for us to play with. One day she picked up a fight with me in one of those one-on-one challenges you could not avoid. I had to accept the challenge. And, o boy, what a fight it was - I ended up the loser! Let's not talk about embarrassment and teasing. Everybody had a field day making jokes at my expense. To redeem myself, I spent the next two years training and preparing mentally for a return fight. I can honourably state here that, the Otabil reputation was successfully redeemed in the next encounter.

When I became an adult, I realized that the determination of who was stronger had major spiritual, moral, physical and financial consequences that would greatly impact on the quality of life I could live and bequeath to my children.

▪ If I was spiritually and morally weak, I would yield to all the enticements to sin around me.

▪ If I was financially weak I may not be able to discharge my responsibilities as a parent.

▪ If I was physically weak I may not have the energy to do all the things I need to do.

▪ If I am relationally weak I will not be able to cultivate the essential relationships I need to accomplish my goals.

I agree that sometimes our weaknesses - especially physical weaknesses - may not be due to our own actions; but I am also aware that we sometimes do things to inflict weakness on ourselves.

It is desirable that we operate from a position of strength instead of weakness. In choosing between the values of Esau and Jacob, we must choose the value that is stronger.

We are so concerned with the question of 'who is stronger?' because that is how we humans have moved ahead throughout the ages. The stronger ones move ahead of the pack whilst the weak struggle to find their place. God said concerning the Esau and Jacob systems that, one of them would be stronger than the other, meaning that one will get ahead of the other. One would have a competitive advantage over the other. It is obvious from what we know so far of the productive values that each of them operated in that, Jacob possessed the stronger value system.

THE ABILITY TO ACCOMPLISH TASKS

Strength refers to the power and ability to accomplish a task. This is not related only to the application of physical force to get a task accomplished, but to all the abilities resident in a person that can be deployed at any time towards the provision of solutions to problems. If you operate from a value system that does not provide you with the strength to overcome the challenges you face, you will find it very difficult to solve your problems. All the problems of life are related to the ratio of strength to the task at hand.

> All the problems of life are related to the ratio of strength to the task at hand.

Lifting a hundred and fifty pound weight will be a major problem for me but a professional heavy weight lifter will lift it with little effort. The issue is not how heavy the load is, but how strong you are. When your strength is little you complain that the problem is too tough and seek to reduce the weight of what you have to lift. There are countless individuals and groups of people who spend precious time and skills working with futility at reducing the weight of what they are required to lift in life. They fail to come to the realization that most weights are not negotiable so the only useful option left to them is to build up on their strength.

IS THE QUESTION WRONG?

One day in a mathematics class I complained to the teacher that the question we were to answer was wrong. I had tried every method I knew to solve the equation without arriving at the answer so I said to the teacher, 'Sir, the question is wrong'. The teacher said to me, 'Otabil, go and work it out again'. I sat for a while, tried what I knew and went back again to the teacher and complained, 'Sir, the question you gave us is wrong; I have used the method you taught us but I am not getting the answer you said we should have'. The teacher just looked at me and said, 'Otabil, you are lazy, there is no problem with the question'. Whilst I stood arguing with my mathematics teacher, he called for one of my classmates to come forward and show his work to me. I moved closer to see my mates work, hoping to find him in the same predicament I was in. I was disappointed. He had arrived at the answer the teacher said we would arrive at. To save my face I retorted, "Sir, this maths problem is too difficult". My teacher looked at me with a measure of pity and said, "Otabil, it's not the problem which is difficult but your mathematics which is weak". I turned with embarrassment and walked back to my desk feeling very stupid. The question was not wrong; it was my strength in mathematics which was weak.

Before you complain about how difficult times have become or how difficult your problem is, think. The problem may not be with the question. It could be your answers which are wrong and not the question. Did you know that somebody somewhere has been able to overcome the challenges you are faced with? Those who constantly complain about the toughness of the question, never discover the toughness of their brains and the creativity of their minds. Successful people are those who had the commitment to answer the questions we were all asking and later turned round to sell us their answers. They develop strength to lift the weight we are all struggling with and then they make a lifetime vocation of showing us how to do what they did. You can also stay and make a commitment to finding answers to the world's questions and market those answers to the world. Pharmaceutical companies all over the world make loads of money by selling us the answers they got after years of experimentation. They simply package their answers in little bottles and sell them to us. Your developed strength is key to your viability on earth. Instead of running out of your present difficulty, stay and answer the questions and then sell us your answers.

> Those who constantly complain about the toughness of the question, never discover the toughness of their brains and the creativity of their minds.

AND THE OLDER SHALL SERVE THE YOUNGER

The second important value judgment that the Lord made concerning the twins was that the older would serve the younger. That was contrary to the value system of the culture they were born into. In the culture that Esau and Jacob were born into, it was the

> Although, there is merit in waiting for our turn patiently, the criterion for who qualifies for earlier service is not necessarily determined by our age but more by our preparedness.

norm for the younger person to serve the older. That is the culture that equates age and seniority with advantage and success. Those who function with this understanding see life as a neat queue with everyone patiently waiting for their turn after the earlier group had been served. Although, there is merit in waiting for our turn patiently, the criterion for who qualifies for earlier service is not necessarily determined by our age, but more importantly by our preparedness. God used the birth of Esau and Jacob to define a new order in which the younger could have an advantage over the older. When He made reference to 'older' and 'younger' the Lord was not referring to their chronological age but more to their attitudinal responses to the ever changing environments they lived in.

■ 'Older' here refers to those who are set in their ways, with what they are familiar and are not ready to explore new and better ways. There are nations and people who are youthful in age and yet have this 'old' attitude to life. They like to stay within the comfort of what has been. For such a group, their reason for living and their response to new challenges has been to hold on to the old and known practices even when the old is incapable of addressing the new problems.

■ 'Younger' refers to those who value the experiences of past practices, but are open to new ideas that will make them more effective and efficient in executing their assignments. They are open to fresh, vibrant and challenging options. There are nations and people who may be older chronologically, but respond to life with this positive upbeat attitude. Age is nothing. Attitude is everything.

At birth, Esau came out first with Jacob following very closely after. Although Jacob was born after Esau was born, he literally takes hold of the heel of Esau as if to say to Esau, 'Don't get overconfident because you came out earlier, I am right behind you'.

The Esaus of this life build their confidence around the fact that they are older, and more experienced. They are the ones who believe that just because they are better educated, they will come out more successfully than others less educated. Esaus are also very comfortable because they started out earlier than the others. They believe leadership will naturally and always be theirs because of their birth, natural or academic positioning. Esaus are set in their old ways and do not easily adapt to new ways and methods. These are the people and nations who pride themselves in their age-old traditions and customs that served a previous generation well. They constantly refer to the past and seek solace in the nostalgia of their past achievements. They forget that the value of the past is to help us build a better future. Their mantra is, 'If these methods worked yesterday, they will always work tomorrow'. How I wish life would be that predictable. The truth is that, life is more robust and unpredictable.

The Jacobs of this life on the other hand, do not allow themselves to be intimidated by the positional advantages of the Esaus. Jacobs say, "Even if you started out first, I will also run my race; even if you have more than I have, I will also build what I have; even if you have more education than I have, I will also strive for excellence". Those with the Jacob disposition do not allow themselves to be intimidated by the obvious historical and positional advantages of Esau.

> Those with the Jacob disposition do not allow themselves to be intimidated by the obvious historical and positional advantages of Esau.

TRADITION VERSUS INNOVATION

In contrast to the Esau attitude of relying on the old systems to solve their problems, the Jacobs possess a younger mindset and are always open to new and fresh ways of solving the old problems. They are aware of the changes around them and constantly explore new paths outside of the old beaten tracks.

- Esau's solve their problems by using the traditional logic and methods of the past to respond to the challenges of the present.

■ Jacobs solve their problems by adapting yesterday's tested and timeless principles to the practicalities of today's ideas.

The contrast between Esau and Jacob is a contest between innovation and tradition. Nations and people who function through the Esau paradigm, routinely and systematically eliminate innovative ideas and the carriers of such ideas from their world. They have no tolerance for those who question the status quo. All the nations in our world that are struggling with development and poverty are also societies that are very intolerant of innovation and social renewal. Such nations limit the options and choices available to them and seek comfort in the tired stories of their ancestors' heroism. They forget that their ancestors were heroes because they innovated in their time to overcome the challenges of their day.

In every vocation of life, we see younger people who manage to get ahead of their older partners. It is not how old you are or who was your senior in class that determines success in life but how well adapted you are to today's challenges. One of the major problems we have in our world today is our over-reliance on seniority based on chronology. Just because someone has been around longer and seen more, does not confer wisdom and valuable experience to that one. The value

> The lesson we learn from Esau and Jacob is that life does not necessarily favour the one who started out first or has natural advantages.

of seniority should be the lessons it teaches us and how it helps us to adapt the principles of the past to the realities of the present. The lesson we learn from Esau and Jacob is that, life does not necessarily favour the one who started out first or has natural advantages. If success were based on who was bigger and older, no little and young person would live a successful and fulfilled life.

BULK VERSUS SPEED

In boxing contests, I have seen people with weight, height and reach advantage as well as the support of a favourable crowd defeated by opponents who appeared less endowed. Muhammad Ali (Cassius Clay as he then was) demonstrated this fact when he challenged Sonny Liston for the world heavyweight title in 1964. Ali went into the fight as an underdog against the terrifying Sonny Liston who had made it a habit of disposing of his opponents with hefty knockout punches. Liston had a bigger muscle and was bulk than Ali and seemed sure to add Ali to his knockout list. When the seventh round bell sounded, Liston did not respond after he had sampled the power and grace of a 'float like a butterfly; sting like a bee' Ali for six rounds. Ali won because he had more speed in his movements than Liston. His feet moved faster, he ducked faster and punched faster. He demonstrated that the ability to move your muscle faster gave you the advantage over the fighter who only packed a good

> Big becomes a liability when it is not complemented with speed.

punch but lacked speed. Big becomes a liability when it is not complemented with speed.

In the epic biblical contest between David and Goliath, the young and agile David defeated the older and slower Goliath. Goliath was so huge and encumbered with such heavy armour that before he got his hand to move to his sword, David had deployed the first deadly shot from his arsenal. In this battle as well as in the Ali-Liston fight, the stronger one was younger, leaner and faster.

Stronger does not imply more mass or bulk. Energy is not just in the availability of mass but in the rate and speed at which that mass can move. When you are heavy and slow, you will be outsmarted by an opponent who has your mass but moves faster than you.

PROCESSING SPEED

In today's economy, the speed that makes us strong is the speed at which we process the bulk of information available to us and how we use the processed information to accomplish tasks assigned to us. It is not so much what you know but how quickly you can translate what you know into what you do. The information age has made it possible for us to have access to large volumes of material through books, newspapers, magazines, radio, television, and the internet. The speed and rapidity at which such information gets to us creates a problem of information overload. It is like a starving man who chances on a huge party of all the foods in the world and decides to consume all that is set before him. You and I know that he will end up dead from over-indulgence. A poor man who has tons of dollar notes dumped on him will end up suffocated by the money he needs. Information overload is a problem now. The challenge today is how to determine junk information from useful information. To do that we have to do five important things.

■ We have to determine our own personal values and beliefs.

■ We have to determine the key areas of our lives that are most important to us

■ We have to determine our life mission and the goals to achieve them

■ We have to determine what information consistent with our values, will help us achieve our life goals

■ We have to sort out the information we need into the important areas of our lives where we function.

I sort out all information into seven major areas of priority in my life. These are, Spiritual growth, family enrichment, pastoral ministry, leadership skills, education programs, entrepreneurial skills and communication skills. These areas of priority define my pursuits and focus. I may once in a while show interest in fields outside these areas but I generally stay within these limits.

MY VALUES

My value system is basically shaped by my Protestant Christian beliefs that affirm faith in God. It is also a belief system that affirms the value of human life and encourages innovation and enterprise. As a result, when sorting data, I look for information that affirms biblical truth and makes them practical for the decisions I make daily. The source of that information may not be directly biblical but if it affirms the harmony of God's self-revelatory and historical dealings with mankind and offers practical insight into my areas of concern, I will pay close attention to them. Any information that repudiates the moral and life imperatives established by biblical truth automatically selects itself out of my reference.

In sorting out the value of information I receive, I make a distinction between the timeless principles of the bible and the practices of people in the bible. For example, the practice of King Solomon, a biblical character, was to marry a thousand women but the principle of the bible is for marriages to be monogamous. I don't blindly follow the practices of people in the bible; I seek out the timeless principles of God. To do that requires a systematic theological enquiry on my part. Please note that you can't be mentally lazy and still find your way out of the maze of life. To make life meaningful we must put our minds to work.

All of us process information through our paradigms. The paradigm you operate from will make all the difference between starvation and satisfaction in the midst of plenty. A paradigm that places little value on invest-

> All of us process information through our paradigms. The paradigm you operate from will make all the difference between starvation and satisfaction in the midst of plenty.

ment and wealth multiplication for example, will always beg from the one who operates from a wealth creation paradigm. When God said one of the twins will be stronger, He was not indicating that the stronger one will be bigger in stature and bulk. Nor was He necessarily inferring that the stronger one will be the one with the greater physical strength. He was referring to the one who had developed the capacity to be *'...swifter than eagles,...stronger than lions'.* **2 Samuel 1:23**

Between Esau and Jacob, different productive cultures and perceptions of life emerged. Those productive cultures and perceptions eventually had very serious implication for subsequent choices they made, and how they positioned themselves in life. As it was with these twins, so it is for us today. The outcome of your life, being shaped by any of these two paradigms, reflects your own responses. You will see how these paradigms influenced the next encounter of the twins.

Chapter 4

THE HUNGRY HUNTER

Now Jacob cooked a stew; and Esau came in from the field, and he was weary. And Esau said to Jacob, "Please feed me with that same red stew, for I am weary."

I n studying the lives and choices of Esau and Jacob, this is what first caught my attention. I had read and re-read their stories from the Bible for so many years and heard so many sermons preached about them. Most of the sermons were very predictable and commented on how Jacob had cheated on his brother for the birthright. I myself had looked at the story of the twins from that point of view until the two verses above caught my attention. Jacob is cooking a stew; Esau is hungry. That took me by surprise. If anyone should be hungry, I thought it should be Jacob because he stayed in the tent and did not go out to hunt for food. Esau the hunter comes out from the field and is hungry whilst Jacob sits in the tent with food. The one who works very hard on the field has no food to eat but the one who stays in the tent is cooking a stew.

This is where the different paradigms of the twins really show. Esau nations and people appear to be the hard working people of the world but never seem to have enough to feed themselves. They work hard on fields such as agriculture, mining, industr, and music, but never seem to have enough to liberate themselves from economic dependency.

■ Those who operate with the Esau paradigm think that the key to a better life is simply to work hard. As a result of that point of view, they focus all their productive priorities on putting in extra hours and effort without ever stopping to think about how to redesign their working structures and arrangements.

■ Esaus always have stories of people who used the methods they are using years ago and succeeded, but never ask themselves whether what worked in the past is suited to today's challenges.

■ Esau nations take so much pride in how much God has blessed them with resources and yet have very little to show for their pride.

Have you noticed that some of the poorest nations in the world are also, strangely, the most richly endowed in natural resources? The land mass of their nations have vast deposits of gold, diamond, oil, platinum, fertile forest and good weather conditions. They also have a large work force of citizens who are ready to sweat in the fields from dawn to dusk for very little pay and yet their presidents and government officials spend much of their time going round begging from nations who do not have a fraction of those natural resources and labour force.

The Esau nations talk this way, "We are endowed with natural resources. We have gold, bauxite, and timber. We feed the world with our natural resources". These are nations, which build their economies on the Esau paradigm of relying on the mass of their natural endowments. They never manage to develop the speed to turn their mass around into real energy that gets the work done. Esau the hunter is hungry; Jacob the tent man is cooking stew.

HUNTING WITHOUT ROASTING

"The lazy man does not roast what he took in hunting."
Proverbs 12:27.

This Biblical wise saying throws light on how we manage the resources we acquire. It describes the disposition of those who do not learn to process their primary products into useful secondary products. There are people who are good at hunting, but do not roast what they hunted for. Roasting is the process that takes hunted meat from its raw state into an edible state.

The reference to 'lazy man' in this proverb does not imply an individual who sits around doing nothing. Many of us are familiar with people who sit around in life and never apply themselves to any demanding activity. That is the usual picture of a 'lazy man'. Because of that image we have of a 'lazy man', when we see people who are involved in an activity we tend to see them as 'hard working' and not lazy. In our minds, a 'hard working' person cannot be a 'lazy man' at the same time. Yet, this verse in the book of Proverbs, describes the 'lazy man' as a hunter. That almost defies our logic of a 'lazy man'. It appears from this verse in proverbs that, there is another qualification for a 'lazy man'.

MENTAL LAZINESS

The definition for the 'lazy man' here is in reference to a hunter who works hard to hunt for game but fails to take his product to the next level. He does not roast what he caught in hunting. So the laziness in question here is not physical laziness but mental laziness. To process or roast what you have into a more valuable product requires a lot of sophisticated thinking.

> To process or roast what you have into a more valuable product requires a lot of sophisticated thinking.

■ Mental laziness is when an individual finds it too mentally tasking to contemplate and explore the possibilities available to him that are beyond his routine.

■ A mind that sits idle and never gets exercised in innovative thinking belongs to a lazy person.

This kind of laziness is very difficult to detect because, most of the people who practice it are very 'hard working' people. Sometimes we call them 'descent hard working' people. They are happy to follow the routine they are familiar with, but will not exert themselves in any mental exercise that is not part of their routine. A lot of us are happy just following the familiar routines and chores of our vocation and never stretch our minds into new fields.

Most 'hard working' pastors, nurses, teachers, mechanics, lawyers, doctors, engineers, secretaries and so on, live from week to week or month to month going from one paycheck to the other. Any time a paycheck comes in, it goes out into expenditure. They have never committed themselves to the task of thinking about how to develop an efficient plan for managing and investing their paycheck in order to increase their income and eventually to stop relying on their paycheck for survival. They do not 'roast' what they took in hunting.

■ *Hunting* is what you do as your profession - singing, building, teaching, selling or providing other services and goods.

■ *Roasting* is what you do with what you gained from your hunting. It is how well you develop what you do and how much you are able to generate from your initial income.

■ *Roasting* helps you to generate secondary income from your primary income.

A corporate organization, nation or individual who does not process what they have into more valuable products can be likened to the lazy hunter who does not process his slaughtered prey beyond its raw state. They work hard on the field and manage to get what they are looking for. It is always the same thing they have been doing for a very long time. They are so good at hunting for their prey that it has become second nature to them. Their hunting instincts are sharp and very predictable, however, they lack the commitment to go to the next level of processing what they hunted for into a value-added product. They do not roast what they took in hunting. If Esau had taken the time to process what he took in hunting from raw meat to consumable food, he would not have begged Jacob for stew.

ROAST WHAT YOU HUNT FOR

Remember the verse, *"The lazy man does not roast what he took in hunting."* For roasting to take place there has to be these conditions.

■ First of all, the slaughtered animal must be dressed. This is where you separate the real meat from the non-edible parts. To dress the meat is to clean the meat. You clean it from all undesirable parts as well as contaminations. It is the process of separating the useful and beneficial from the parts that are not useful and beneficial.

■ Secondly, the meat is spiced. To spice is to take the scent and taste of rawness from your product. For the product to be attractive on the market, it must be free from rawness.

■ The third stage is to put the meat on fire. The fire represents the pressure and the heat that transforms raw meat into eatable meat. The kind of pressure required to take your product to the next level could come from your customers, competitors or the quality control office. This kind of pressure provides you with the fire to process your product into a more desirable commodity.

Roasting takes place when we take what we have in the raw state through a process that transforms it from a simple raw item into a sophisticated and useful item. The heat for roasting could also be likened to the pressure for new training and skill development you put yourself through in order to increase your value.

1. Roasting also requires constant turning in order not to burn one side of a piece of meat whilst the other sides remain raw and uncooked.

2. The turning of the meat represents the constant changes and repositioning that is required to make us always good for the market. What you know today may not be sufficient for what you want to do tomorrow.

Both burnt and raw meat are not fit for consumption in much the same way as both raw and over-exposed talents and products have little market value. Sometimes people spend too much time perfecting just one area of their lives and totally ignore other complementary areas of their lives. Specialization is very good, but it is very vital that we develop the complementary skills that will enhance what we have specialized in. As a pastor, I specialize in preaching but I spend time developing the complementary skills of leadership and management to make me more effective.

Those who only focus all their energy to specialize in only one area without complementary skills end up burnt. Whilst there are people who burn only one side of the meat, there are those who never cook or process what they have. Everything they have is in a state of rawness and as such, unfit for direct consumption by the people they serve. There are musicians with raw talent who have not been able to turn their talents into valuable skills. When they play an instrument or sing, their talent just shines through, but their unprofession-alism obscures the shine on their talent. The talent is there but it has not been roasted. Roasting processes what we work hard for, from its state of rawness into an edible state.

Roasting takes what is hunted for, to the next level of processing, in order to add value to it. It operates from the understanding that the potential for productivity is unlimited because, it is based on how effectively we are able to turn around what has been hunted for. If the hunter hunts for meat and wants it eaten, it must first go through a process of roasting.

- Roasting adds value to your product. The extent of processing we give to a product determines the extent of its usefulness and value.

- Roasting makes it possible for the usefulness of a product to be preserved for a long time. It adds shelf-life to a product and gives the hunter the opportunity to bargain for a better life.

- Roasting makes the product a direct consumable product.

The immediate context in which roasting takes place is in the area of meat processing, but the principle has wider application to almost all endeavours of man. Whether it is in talent development or in commodity processing, the principle cuts across all endeavours. I have come across many decent hard-working people who live on the edge of economic survival because they were not 'roasting' people. They produced through the routine they are used to, but do not take their products to the next level of production. They do not have the mental commitment to seek ways to add value to their primary products.

A typical nation which operates with a productive culture that only produces primary commodities may produce gold, for example, but will have no facility for "roasting" the gold. There is no gold refinery. They are good at producing the raw gold. As a matter of fact, they are so proud of how much gold they have that it becomes part of their own self-description. The problem though, is that, since they cannot refine what they produce, they end up taking their gold to another nation which has a refinery to refine the gold and make expensive pretty jewelry. When the people of the gold producing nation needs jewelry, guess what? They go to the nation with the refinery to buy at a price so much higher than the raw gold they produced. These are hard working nations with a development paradigm of producing raw material, but lack the commitment to process what they have to the next level.

> Those who do not roast what they took in hunting, stay at the level of rawness.

Those who do not roast what they took in hunting, stay at the level of rawness. They may have raw talents in music, but will not commit themselves to the mental discipline that will enable them to 'roast' their talents into marketable skills. They have raw talents in sports but do not roast or process the talents into winning skills on the field of play. There are preachers with the 'anointing' to preach, who never develop their communication skills beyond the 'anointing' they received from the Lord.

PRIMARY PRODUCERS.

Primary producers produce things in their natural state with very little improvement. Secondary producers make several products out of that same product. For example, a primary producing nation may simply produce oil out of its land or sea resources for export. That is what hunters do. They produce out of what is naturally available. One paradigm will be to drill the crude oil from the earth, whereas the other paradigm will focus on refining it into gasoline, heating oil, kerosene, plastics, textile fibers, coatings, adhesives, drugs, pesticides, and fertilizers. Jacobs take simple products and make them into industries.

It is amazing the kind of industries people are able to spin out of simple talents and abilities. Sports men and women of today are producing more from their abilities than their predecessors did. Years ago, basketball players only entertained people on the field of play shooting hoops. Now, most of them have processed their talents and skills into major industries. They spin off clothes, fragrances, television appearances, musical productions, book sales and advertising endorsements out of the primary skills they have and display on the playing field. Soccer stars, track and field athletes and other sports professionals have all managed to turn their talents into industries. That is the Jacob paradigm.

"Now Jacob cooked a stew and Esau came in from the field and he was weary".

Jacob cooked a stew. He was not a man of the field but he cooked stew whiles the man of the field was hungry. Esau came from the field. He had been gone since morning to work hard, running after rabbits and deer for the whole day. He had spent much of the day alone, sweating on the fields and trying hard to make a living so he can probably return home with a kill. However, when he got home from work that evening, he had nothing to eat. He turned around and saw his brother Jacob who never went to the field, eating a very tasty meal.

The hunter was hungry. The tent man was eating. The Jacob and Esau paradigm reflects the conditions of people today. The Jacobs stay in their tents to process what they have and always have enough to eat and to negotiate for better conditions.

Before Esau and Jacob were born, God had indicated that one would be stronger than the other. The Jacob system is always stronger than the Esau system. When an organization or an individual operates with the paradigm that does not process its resources to generate greater benefit, they are happy and pride themselves in the raw materials they produce. They never stop to think that, they later buy the processed finished products made out of their raw materials at a higher price. Many third world Nations are trapped in this kind of economy. They work so hard to produce items such as gold, only to export them in their raw state to the industrialized nations who process the raw materials into finished products which they in turn sell back to the third world nations at higher cost. A nation becomes 'third world' if it does not have the capacity to manage its resources from the raw primary product stage to the sophisticated processed stage. Such a nation will always struggle to catch up on its current deficits with its competitor nations who possess the capacity to process products to their varied refined stages.

> A nation becomes 'third world' if it does not have the capacity to manage its resources from the raw primary product stage to the sophisticated processed stage.

It is not only nations who struggle to catch up on this kind of deficit in their dealings with others, but individuals also suffer similar deficits in their dealings. The individual who is simply pleased because he has the capacity to produce, but does not look at the possibilities of production inherent in what he is doing, will also be running a personal deficit. Any individual who sees his or her salary as spending money alone will always run a personal deficit in his or her finances. Your salary is what you got out of your hunt. After you receive it you must find ways of making it work for you beyond the month. That may mean that you study the investment options available to you to increase the value of your money. Each one of us must ask ourselves these five simple questions:

- What do I have?

- What can I do with what I have - will I consume or invest it?

- Can I get more from what I have than what I am now getting?

- Does what I possess have the capacity for more value than what it is now?

- Do I have the information and skills to increase the value of what I have?

- Do I have the patience to nurture what I have into a more valuable product?

Your honest answers to these questions will help you discover the potential inherent in what is in your hand today and what is required to realize that potential.

Remember that your gifts and talents can achieve far more than simply earning you a regular salary. Even after you earn a salary, you must note that your income has more possibilities than just to pay for your bills.

Savings on your salary over a period of time could grow into the capital you require for a significant investment. When you see what your little savings can become in the next ten years, you will not despise the littleness of what you have now. You can use the Jacob value system to stretch the potential of what you have in your hand today, into enormous value for your future use.

THIS BOOK IS A PROCESSED PRODUCT

There are many spin-offs that we can produce out of our primary products. For example, the book you are reading now is a spin-off from a single message I received inspiration to preach. The inspiration came from God to preach the message. That is the primary stage. I could have been pleased that I had been faithful to God and preached the message he gave me. When I preached the message first to my congregation, it was for free and there was no commercial benefit in it for me. I had to later sit down to stretch and flesh out the message, spice it and process it into a book. For it to become a book, I had to go beyond the simple message I first preached. That called for mental discipline and commitment to do further research. I had to take time to develop the initial ideas of the message better and to incorporate new insights which I had not considered when I first delivered the raw material. Now you hold in your hand a book which includes my thoughts on this subject, in a far better form than I first received and preached it. While I did not earn any money directly on the original sermon, it is likely I might receive royalties on the value I added to the original sermon which is now in a book form.

FAITHFULNESS IS INCREASING THE
VALUE OF WHAT YOU HAVE

In the parable of the talents, Jesus taught that faithfulness is not the ability to preserve what you have, but the ability to increase the value of what you have. Investing what you have to increase its value is more worthy than preserving what you have in the state you received it.

There are people who operate on the paradigm of simply working hard to keep things as they are and think they are being faithful to God. They criticize anyone who wants to make much out of the little they have and sometimes even consider such people as too materialistic. Such people may have the shock of their lives when the Lord says to them, 'you wicked and lazy servant... you could have put my talents in a bank and earned some profit on it' **Matthew 25: 26-27** . That is the attitude of the Lord towards those who receive His abilities and resources and just content themselves with preservation without innovation and increase. God does not accept from us what He gave to

> God does not accept from us what He gave to us in the same state as it was when He gave it to us. When God gives us talents, He only recognizes and commends the value we add to it.

us in the same state as it was when He gave it to us. When God gives us talents, He only recognizes and commends the value we add to it.

The Esau system makes us build our personal and corporate economies on unsophisticated rudimentary primary products while the Jacob system relies on sophisticated, refined and processed products. It is from this basic difference in productive culture that both Esau and Jacob go ahead to negotiate their future.

■ Their paradigms determine how they manage their resources.

■ How they manage their resources determines how they negotiate with others.

When Esau meets Jacob at the negotiating table the outcomes are different for both of them. One uses what he has produced for consumption in the present to negotiate for and buys the future; the other, because he has nothing to eat in the present, sells the future to buy the present. What are you negotiating for and buying?

Chapter 5

Jacob negotiates with his prepared stew Esau negotiates on empty stomach

But Jacob said, "Sell me your birthright as of this day." And Esau said, "Look, I am about to die; so what is this birthright to me?"

This is where the negotiation between Esau and Jacob takes place. There are two definitions for the word 'negotiate' in *Webster's Random Dictionary*, which are important for what we are talking about;

1. To deal or bargain with another or others, as in the preparation of a treaty or contract or in preliminaries to a business deal.

2. To move through, around, or over in a satisfact-
    ory manner: e.g. *to negotiate a difficult dance
    step without tripping: to negotiate sharp curves.*

Those two definitions can be fused into one thought.
The ideas implied in them are complementary. In almost
all negotiations those two ideas happen because every
negotiation is a deal with implications and consequences. Every deal we make in a negotiation must help
us to satisfactorily manoeuvre our way around various
difficult phases of our lives. There are negotiations we
do in the boardroom and others we do daily in our
choices. Boardroom negotiations are very familiar to us.
They are formal and normally happen in corporate settings. Soap operas and movies have taken us into many
boardrooms to observe the intrigues of corporate negotiations and takeovers so much so that many of us have
become familiar with all the plots and counter-plots
which play out in those scenes - at least the glamorised
versions. But most negotiations happen in our daily
lives and in very informal settings.

WE NEGOTIATE DAILY

Informal negotiations happen from the day you are
born till the day you die. Your birth was influenced by
the negotiation between your father and mother.
Sometimes it is a loving negotiation; other times it is a
hasty, guilt ridden negotiation with a lot of pain and
bitter consequences. Informal negotiations happen

among kids on the play ground, husband and wife, among siblings, in the classroom, on the sports field, at the dinning table, behind our television screens whilst watching our favourite show and in every conceivable place that human beings find themselves. Most negotiations are focused on who will get a better deal. Every negotiation is a 'give and take' affair. You offer what you have, for what you need. Sometimes you negotiate with yourself; other times you negotiate with other people.

> Every negotiation is a 'give and take' affair. You offer what you have for what you need.

A good negotiation should leave everybody a winner because both parties have a good value system and seek for transactions that will have beneficial consequences for their future. Sometimes, one person wins and the other loses because whilst one had his long-term value in mind, the other was just seeking for short-term pleasure. Other times both parties lose because their negotiations were based on narrow self interest.

The negotiation of Esau and Jacob was an informal negotiation. One party - Jacob - had a good value system. The other party - Esau- had a wrong value system. There was no boardroom, no nice suits, no elegant furniture, no lawyers or special aides. It was just two brothers sitting out on their family compound and talking about food. As innocuous as the setting and circumstances were, the outcome of that short and simple encounter determined the future fortunes of those brothers and a lot of other people who would live thousands of years after them. Significant moments of history are sometimes determined under very ordinary circumstances.

THE NEGOTIATION SCENARIO

The scene was very plain and ordinary. Esau comes home from the field hungry after a hard day's work and sees Jacob eating. It was bad enough for Esau to have had no food prepared after he returned from the field. In addition to that liability, he actually proceeded to ask for the prepared food of Jacob.

> Significant moments of history are sometimes determined under very ordinary circumstances.

May be he expected free dinner from Jacob. He probably even felt Jacob owed him a meal. Maybe over the years he had made it a habit of coming home to eat Jacob's stew after a hard day's work. Probably, he did not understand that the Jacob paradigm was very different from his own paradigm. He had not noticed that Jacob operated a value-oriented paradigm which made him look out for good transactions to increase his worth. Anyone who negotiates with a Jacob must be careful of what they ask for.

DO YOU WANT THE MEAL OR THE RECIPE?

Esau's request is very instructive. He says to Jacob, *'give me some of the same stew you are eating'*. He wanted the same 'roasted' resources of Jacob in its processed form.

■ He was not looking for fire to cook his own food; neither was he even looking for the recipe of Jacob's stew.

■ He was not looking for the ingredients of Jacob's stew. He just wanted the processed food of Jacob.

■ He wanted the finished product and not the means to process his raw hunted game into edible food.

Esau desired to partake of Jacob's success without considering its possible cost. There are people like that; as well as nations. We've all met them before. Those who are so desperate to fit in and be part of the show but are not ready to learn their own lines well. They want a piece of everybody's action for free. They want to eat what belongs to others and quickly satisfy their need immediately. They have no time and the discipline to get the recipe for what they desire and cook it themselves.

What Esau had not counted on was that those who use time and skill to process raw material into finished products have a high price for their goods and services. They don't sell their wares cheaply. They normally have greater advantage in mind when they sell you what they have. As a good steward of the resources God had given him, Jacob was not about to give out for free what he had worked hard to produce. If all of us gave out what we produced freely, I wonder how we could ever get remunerated for the production of our goods and services.

Esau wanted the finished product of hot spicy succulent stew, so Jacob made out a good offer for the product he was asking for. He asked Esau for something that immediately did not appear valuable. He asked for the birthright of Esau as the trade off for the prepared food. Jacob did not want food from Esau he only wanted the birthright.

THE BIRTHRIGHT

What is the birthright? In the culture of Esau and Jacob, the birthright was the benefits a child received by virtue of their birth and heritage. Esau was the first-born son of his father Isaac and as such, was first in line to receive the blessing of the family's inheritance. Isaac himself had received it from his father Abraham, and was duty bound by tradition to transfer it to his first-born son.

- The birthright was not given until at the time the father was ready to die.

- It was always in the future.

- It was not materially visible to both Esau and Jacob.

- It was an unseen empowerment that allowed a person to excel above their contemporaries.

Who ever had the birthright of the first son, had access to unique abilities and opportunities. It was not something that had been inherited, rather it was something that was yet to be inherited. Jacob's stew which Esau wanted, was however not in the future; it was right there and present. It could be seen with the naked eyes and it could be eaten right away. The birthright was in the future; the stew was in the present.

- Whilst Esau was seeking for what was present now, Jacob wanted what would be available in the future.

- Esau wanted what was already processed, Jacob wanted that which would enable him to possess the leadership of the future.

- Esau wanted the seen, Jacob wanted the unseen.

Hungry people have intense present need and as such, close their eyes to the consequences of their choices. Esau said, 'I want the food now, I am weary, I am hungry'. He was throwing tantrums. 'Give me, give me, give me; now, now, now'. When people are desperate for instant gratification, they have little patience for wisdom, tact and good judgment.

> Hungry people have intense present need and as such close their eyes to the consequences of their choices.

Esau had no value for his future inheritance. He was

more concerned with his present need and hunger than with his future inheritance.

When people become desperate for self-gratification in any area of endeavour, their own hunger becomes a trap to them. Any good negotiator will tell you that over zealous and eager traders easily get burnt in negotiations. Good negotiators, do not say yes to the first offer or counter-offer. They are careful to mask their own need with calmness. They always have their future objectives in mind and seek for opportunities that will help them access those objectives. Anytime you have to negotiate an important phase of your life, be guided by these important considerations from the encounter of Esau and Jacob. Whether the choices you have to make have to do with dropping out of school because of financial need; getting sexually involved with someone you are not married to, choosing a marriage partner, transacting a business arrangement, choosing your career path or seeking the path for fulfillment, these lessons from Esau and Jacob can be very helpful.

1. Don't negotiate on empty stomach

Because Esau was hungry and weary he felt he was at the point of death and had to have Jacob's stew.

- The Esaus in this life negotiate when they are hungry.

- The Jacobs of this life negotiate when they are full.

■ Esaus feel constantly under pressure to have a need met.

■ Jacobs even when they are desperate act with calm assurance and confidence when pursuing what they need.

Let me give you free advice: don't negotiate when you are hungry and starved. Every state of emptiness you feel as you negotiate all the various phases of your life, makes you vulnerable and open to manipulation.

2. Don't negotiate when you are tired

Weariness and tiredness make you long for relief. It is like walking for a long time in very uncomfortable shoes. Your feet get tired. Your body gets weary. At that time, all that occupies your mind is getting to a place where you can take off your shoes. When you enter through the doors of your home what do you do? Before you do anything else, you take off your shoes. The need to find relief is very over-powering. The need to find relief can be so over-powering that, it takes the center stage in all your thinking and dominates your faculties of reasoning and judgment. When Esau came from the field not only was he hungry, he was also very tired. He was weary. He needed rest and relief very quickly. In that state of weariness, he was ready to give in to anything Jacob was demanding in order to get his relief.

Sometimes through a combination of domestic, office and spiritual pressure, we become so desperate for various reliefs that for the moment nothing seems to matter more than having the relief we are looking for. The man who feels harassed in his marriage can get to the point of seeking relief from any woman who would listen. If that woman does not only want to be the sounding board of a frustrated husband, the conse-quences for the man's marriage will be very precarious. People get so harassed by their creditors that they seek relief from more severe lending conditions and other people who sense their desperation and give them worse loan terms. I am yet to see a desperate person looking for relief, make an informed and intelligent choice. My counsel to you is simple – don't pressurize yourself with your problems. All problems have a life cycle and an expiry date. Keep your perspectives right.

> All problems have a life cycle and an expiry date. Keep your perspectives right.

3. Call for time out

When the pressure of your situation gets to you during any negotiation, it is helpful to pause, stay calm, and reprocess your thoughts and options. In a formal nego-tiation setting, you could ask for a time out and take a therapeutic walk to recharge your batteries. You will be surprised how a little time off can help clear your head. In the informal negotiation setting that occurs daily in our lives you could take time away from the source of your crisis to retreat and pray for God's guidance. That retreat alone is a major victory if you can do it.

It will not help your case to let the adrenalin of the

moment drive you into a rushed decision. Remember that any flow of adrenalin in your body, also helps to distort your sense of judgment. The combined effects of stress, anxiety and frustration will release in your body, the hormones that make you feel like running or hastening. When you find yourself in that state, take time off to be calm and rethink. That is what Esau should have done. When Jacob made the offer to buy his birthright for a dinner plate, he should have sensed that something was going wrong somewhere.

In a negotiation, silence can be a powerful weapon. If Esau had kept silent for a while it could have turned the pressure from him to Jacob to look again at his offer. The silence of Esau would have made Jacob offer a more reasonable bargain chip. But Esau was so frustrated by his own hunger and the cheeky calmness of Jacob that he blurted out, 'What is the birthright to me?'.

> In a negotiation silence can be a powerful weapon.

Many people speak too quickly during negotiations and give away much in anger. It was obvious that Esau was angry. Who was he angry with? Probably with himself and his sense of powerlessness.

4. Don't respond to the provocation

God who created us, also endowed us with the power of reciprocity. That means that we give back to people out of what we receive from them. When people are nice to us, we tend to respond back in the same nice way. When people frown, we respond with a frown. So most of the time, our moods are a simple reflection of the moods around us. You can be provoked to make decisions that will cost you dearly in the future.

The implication of that attitude is that, people can easily control our moods and actions if they know how to do so. If somebody wants you to be impatient, he can do that by acting irritated and impatient with you. At a formal negotiating table for example, people can make irritating offers to you or keep tapping on the table to suggest that they don't have time to waste. If you pick up on their signals, you will rush into making a decision that can trap you for a long time to come.

Reacting to the provocation of your opponent, limits you to the emotions he allows you to express. When Esau came out from the field and saw Jacob looking fresh and satisfied it is possible it made him feel angry and irritated. Here he was, having worked so hard and all Jacob was doing was cooking and enjoying a good meal. He was angry that Jacob was satisfied. Esau was hungry and agitated; Jacob was satisfied and at rest with himself. Then Esau asks for Jacob's stew. Jacob calmly, without any sense of haste or urgency, demands the birthright. It was quite a simple request, 'give me your birthright'. Esau is angry with the situation and screams, 'what is the birthright to me when I am dying?'. That retort was a direct play back from the tone set by Jacob.

A wiser response would have been to regard Jacob's

> Reacting to the provocation of your opponent, limits you to the emotions he allows you to express.

offer with disdain and walked on towards Rebecca's kitchen. Or he could have stayed on to negotiate Jacob's stew for a goat he had brought from the farm or something close to that.

5. Value what you have

Esau's retort, 'what is the birthright to me?' is very revealing. He undervalued his own strength and worth. It is dangerous to devalue your worth before someone who is in negotiation with you. Woe on you when your opponent places more value on your treasure than you do yourself. Many individuals and organisations have entered into negotiations with a very low value for what they had to offer and ended up releasing their birthright for almost nothing.

> Woe on you when your opponent places more value on your treasure than you do yourself

It is very easy to devalue what you have because of familiarity and commonness. When you live with something for so long and always have access to it, you tend to take it for granted. I was a good artist when I was young - I still am. When I was young, I would sit around and just sketch with my pencil on paper and have adults stand around amazed at what I could draw. But I just saw it as nothing. After I had finished drawing, I would erase what I had done to the protestations of those around. To them, what I had done was a work they would wish to keep; for me it was nothing because I could do it again anytime I wanted. What they valued, I took for granted. It happens in marriages, churches and friendships; we easily take for granted what we have around us all the time. Esau said, 'what is the birthright to me?' He had grown up with the knowledge that he would inherit the birthright as natural consequence of his life that, the import of it had been lost on him. He took his most treasured asset for granted. I hope that is not your attitude towards God, your family, gifts, talents and abilities.

When you sit before an interviewing panel make sure that your future employer does not see more talent in you than you think you have. When he gets to think that you don't know what you are worth, he could offer you a flattering service package, which he knows is far lower than our worth. People get flattered by so little because they don't appreciate the true value of what God has endowed them with. All of us sell things by our perceived value of the object.

6. Don't exaggerate your need

When Jacob made his offer, Esau, responded, 'I am about to die...' You and I know he was not about to die. The hunger was painful and tough but he was nowhere near dying. What Esau did was simple; he exaggerated his need. People who exaggerate their own need, make drastic choices to solve them. They make their situation so desperate that they look for desperate solutions. If a young man feels his poverty is worse than death, he will take a gun and attempt to rob a bank. If he sees the poverty as a reversible situation, he will find constructive ways to change his circumstances. He would think of getting a college degree or learning a trade that will better his employment chances.

A young girl who sees a pimple on her nose one morning may decide not to go to school that day because she would look 'weird'. If she knew that all people her age have pimples and that pimples are not permanent, she would overlook her plight and go to school. An older single woman who thinks marriage is the most important state for her, may worry herself into depression, looking for a husband.

Esau raised the stakes of the negotiations when he said, '*I am about to die*'. For a person who thinks he is about to die, birthrights and their benefits become meaningless. When you pressurize yourself into desperation, you will sell yourself cheap.

> When you pressurize yourself into desperation, you will sell yourself cheap.

Negotiators who exaggerate their need, minimize their own options and choices.

7. Negotiate the offer down

Many Africans practice very good negotiating skills daily. Whenever we visit the market, charter a taxi or buy any goods and services we practice this skill. Traders deliberately hike their prices with the full expectancy that the buyer will negotiate for a more favourable price.

Negotiators, who sell products and services, deliberately make very high offers because they expect their offers to be negotiated down. Esau could easily have negotiated down the offer of Jacob. It was not a take it or leave it situation. And even if it was, there were so many other opportunities available to him to have the dinner he needed for almost no price at all. He could have walked by Esau, into the kitchen of their mother Rebecca. He could have gone to a neighbour's for his meal or just waited for another 30 minutes to cook his own meal. Why did he not consider all these options? It is in the response he gave, 'what is this birthright to me?' He so devalued his own treasure that he did not feel any need to negotiate down Jacob's expensive offer.

8. Buy the future

Jacob trades with Esau not to maintain what he has, but to gain what he did not have. He exchanges what is seen for what is not seen. He trades present possession for the opportunity of the future. He wants to take hold of the vision of the future. The present terrain is not enough for Jacob because in his mind he sees pictures of new possibilities ahead. Taking hold of the future is more important to Jacob than simply keeping what he has been able to process and attain to now.

Jacob knows where the future opportunities will be located. He sees ahead and projects strategically into days yet unborn.

Jacob does not wait for the future to happen before he starts planning and thinking about his next moves. He anticipates trends and triggers the activities that will precipitate the future. Jacobs know the difference between what is good, what is important and what is most important. They have a discerning mind that can tell the difference in value of items and situations placed before them. They have a keen sense of true value. They can discover precious gems in the gutter.

WHERE IS THE FUTURE?

There are three realities of time - past, present and the future. The past and the future occurs in the mind. The past is a memory. The future is an imagination. These two expressions of time occurs in the mind. The reality of the past is in our memories of what has already happened. The reality of the future is in how we imagine things will happen. The past is very powerful because it is the only expression of time that has already happened and therefore the only one which imprints itself on our minds. The present is reality that is still unfolding, as such, it can be observed and appreciated. The future on the other hand has not happened. So it has no reference point.

> The past and the future occur in the mind. The past is a memory. The future is an imagination.

Most people's lives consist of their memories of the past and their observation of the present. Such people respond only to what has happened and what is happening. They are reactive to life's choices and not proactive. They feel powerless to change what they don't like in their own lives and often lack the courage to question their choices.

The future, however, belongs to those who use their mind to design what should happen after today. Those who are able to harness the power of forward looking imagination are able to set out what the future would be like. They are the ones who buy the future with today's currency. Such people are proactive and do not wait to respond after things have happened. Jacob belonged to this group. He used the power of imagination to buy the future.

Creative imagination is the ability to see and know what will happen in the next twenty years ahead of time. It is through the power of forward-looking imagination that innovations are conceived and birthed. Many of today's successful people saw the future and bought it ahead of time when others only sought comfort in the past and observed the present. Today's scientific reality was yesterday's science fiction. Those who understand the value of tomorrow, use the resources and opportunities of today to negotiate for and purchase the future.

The future of a Nation does not only reside in the traditions that kept them through their past struggles but more than anything else, in the ability of the people to use the principles of those traditions to create a new world they do not see.

THE FUTURE IS CHEAP.

Any one who can anticipate which company's investments will have the highest value in the next ten years, can buy into those investments today at a relatively cheap price. If you knew which real estate would be most expensive in the next twenty years, you could buy it very cheap today. By careful observation of historical evidence, Jacob knew what the blessing of the birthright had done for his father Isaac. The history of Abraham his grandfather and Isaac his father helped him to determine what was important in his life. God called Abraham and blessed him greatly. Before he died, Abraham transferred the blessing to his son Isaac. Jacob knew that as a result of the birthright, his father Isaac had prospered tremendously as an immigrant worker in a hostile nation. As a result of that keen sense of history, Jacob knew the future belonged to the one who possessed the blessing of the birthright. How much does the future cost? Simply, the value of the future is in the eyes of the keen observer. Value is in the eyes of the beholder.

THE PRESENT IS EXPENSIVE

Those who wait to eat the present after it has already been cooked, pay the highest premium for their taste. When you wait till a location becomes famous before you think of buying real estate there, you will pay top dollar for it. When you wait to be nice to people only after they become famous, you pay a high price to have access to them. Those who desire to eat Jacob's stew pay a high price for it. Esau had to pay top price for Jacob's already cooked stew. He paid for present satisfaction with his future potential. All that he was capable of becoming was used to buy one dinner meal that was well cooked and ready to be

> Those who desire to eat Jacob's stew pay a high price for it.

eaten. I have heard many sermons preached that sought to portray Jacob as a thief and a manipulator of Esau in this transaction. I am yet to find any scriptural proof for that assumption. Jacob certainly had his faults, but in this transaction, his position was more honourable.

When Jacob made the offer to sell his stew for the birthright of Esau, there was no counter offer. There was no attempt to renegotiate. There was no stalemate. There was no pause. There was no reconsideration. Can you imagine that? Somebody makes an offer to buy your future inheritance and treasure for one dinner serving and there is no effort to renegotiate. Esau simply refers to his present desperation and need as his critical concern. He was aware of the value of the birthright in the culture he grew up in, yet, in his moment of need nothing was valuable again. Morality is no longer important, future dreams are no longer exciting. The only thing that matters to Esau is the satisfaction of his present hunger. What a depraved character.

Without a keen sense of history and value, we will always sell our greatest values for the fulfillment of today's demands.

Esau bought the finished product and paid dearly for it. I have always wondered why he did not at least settle for a deal where Jacob would feed him dinners for the rest of his life. Certainly that would have been a less unwise deal. Not the best but certainly better than selling your future for one dinner meal. Have you ever considered what you have been giving away in order to indulge in your present pleasures? When Esaus and Jacobs negotiate, the Esaus almost always come out the losers.

ESAU SELLS THE FUTURE

Esau failed to develop what he had for the crucial negotiation with Jacob. Because he had nothing in the present, he could only sell his future. I see this logic replicated over and over as I observe human behaviour. I have seen nations sell off their rain forest as timber for a pittance just to survive their present economic hardships. As an African, one of the sorest and most emotive events of my history has to do with the Trans-Atlantic Slave Trade and its effects on my race. I have spent years reading the history of that very painful era and visited sites that memorialise that event. It has been called the 'African Holocaust'. It is the most horrifying event in human history over the last thousand or so years when greed and cruelty from Europe, the Americas and Africa converged to ravage the souls of the young African men and women.

The soreness of my grief is centered around the question of how Africans could sell their own for processed commodities from Europe. Much as I hold the European merchants responsible for their low regard for the sanctity of human life, the real question I ask myself is, 'How could our African forebearers ever imagine that human life was equivalent to rum, sugar and guns from Europe?' Why did they not continue to trade in processed commodities with their European counterparts? I address those questions to Africa because I cannot change the European; I can only change me. If we had not sold, they would not have bought! Europe sold us their processed present commodities and we sold them our future. We used the lives and destinies of our young men and women to pay for the satisfaction of our taste buds! As I look around at the present difficulties of the African continent, I ask myself whether the premise for our trade relations with other nations has changed in structure from the one which led millions of our people into slavery? If we don't redesign the structure of our productive paradigm we will repeat the horrors of our past. Today our rain forest is gone. Our wild life is gone. Our land mass lies fallow from the over-exploitation of foreign-owned mining companies. Our rivers are poisoned with unchecked dumping of waste. Our young men and women are leaving our nations to labour and build other civilizations. The future is being sold again.

THE ESAU WAY IS A PROFANE WAY

On our television screens, we see the haunting images of naturally well resourced nations whose citizens have been reduced to living skeletons. Those living skeletons are the trophies of bad leaders of nations which have neither reason nor justification to be poor. Prodigal leaders who waste a nation's resources on senseless political vendetta and the amassing of personal wealth, which is acquired by just selling off their nations natural resources to fill up their foreign accounts. That is the profane way of Esau.

This is how the Lord admonishes us to be careful with

our choices *"....lest there be any fornicator or profane person like Esau, who for one morsel of food sold his birthright. For you know that afterward, when he wanted to inherit the blessing, he was rejected, for he found no place for repentance, though he sought it diligently with tears."* **Hebrews 12:16-17**

The verse above describes Esau as a fornicator and a profane person. A fornicator is one who takes that which is precious and sells it cheaply. A profane person takes that which is noble and honourable and dishonours it. That is the Esau way. They don't add value to what they have; they actually operate in ways that devalue what they have. I think the reason most people sympathize with Esau is because their paradigms are closer to Esau's.

> A profane person takes that which is noble and honourable and dishonours it.

The world has seen people with great talent and potential go waste because of self-gratifying choices. Our news media have chronicled the stories of preachers, sportsmen and women, politicians, entertainers, students, professors, chief executives, military officers and various talented and skilled professionals in all fields of life who have on occasion, traded their great achievements and honour for very dubious and prodigal choices. After God gives a nation all the gold, silver, oil and a fertile land, is it not profaning the endowments of God to abuse those resources and just go round borrowing from less naturally endowed nations? After God gives us all those unique talents and gifts to use to serve our generation, is it not profaning the gifts of God to trade them cheaply for instant gratification? The Esau way is a profane way.

Chapter 6

DO YOU UNDERSTAND WHAT YOU JUST SIGNED?

❖❖❖❖❖

Then Jacob said, "Swear to me as of this day." So he swore to him, and sold his birthright to Jacob.

Reading is not the same as comprehension. Looking is not the same as seeing. Hearing is not the same as understanding. Reading, looking and hearing are all superficial. They are not deep enough. You can do all those three things without getting the import and meaning of what you are considering. I have read books on astro-physics from cover to cover and not understood a hundredth of what was being discussed.

> Reading is not the same as comprehension. Looking is not the same as seeing. Hearing is not the same as understanding.

I could read the book because it was written in English,

but I could not understand because the meaning was in physics. I have sometimes sat in front of people and heard them speak for minutes and never remembered what they were saying because my mind could not follow the logic and structure of their ideas. I have sometimes passed by people I knew without recognizing them because I was in deep thought over something else. Just because you can read a legal document in English does not mean you understand all of its legal intentions and implications. Esau assumed that just because he understood the language of his transaction with Jacob, he knew the meaning and long-term implications of what was said.

THE LAW CAN BE YOUR PROTECTOR

After negotiating a good deal, the law can be your best protector. A legal seal to your transaction protects what you have agreed on, from future uncertainties. It preserves your thoughts and efforts from those who would like to unjustly steal from you. To a very large extent, the legal instrument you use to protect both your intellectual and property rights are the only guarantees you can have that those rights will benefit you in the future. The Jacobs of this world are always very careful to protect their deals and transactions with a legal agreement. When in negotiation with a Jacob, he will seek to put on paper what you have both agreed, to be sure both of you have the same meaning of what is written.

THE POWER OF AN OATH

Within the culture of Esau and Jacob, the most binding commitment to a deal was to swear to each other and pledge commitment to the fulfillment of that pledge. They did not have law courts and the legal instruments we have in our society today. However, they had great reverence for God and the oaths people entered into. Many times in the bible, oaths were sworn as the guarantee for transactions made. They were aware that when two people uttered a vow to each other, they bound themselves to an oath before God and that anyone who broke such a vow incurred serious consequences from the Lord.

When Jacob told Esau to swear to him after the deal was agreed on, he was guaranteeing and protecting his future. Jacob knew the nature of reckless people who in moments of desperation will agree to a deal and later renege because the consequences of their choice now stares them in the face. He was very sure that Esau was going to feel remorse for the decision he had just made, so he committed him there and then to an irrevocable agreement. Swearing to a vow in the days of Jacob is equivalent to signing a legal agreement in our days. The oath was declared on earth and it was settled in heaven. Within the context of the two parties agreeing and binding themselves to a condition here on earth, those conditions were binding also in heaven. That is how legally and spiritually binding an oath was.

Anyone who desires to function in the Jacob paradigm, must not take any legal arrangement lightly.

When you are impressed upon to append your signature to any legal document, you must ascertain that the provisions in that document are representative of your own wishes.

WATCH WHAT YOU SIGN

Our generation has inherited a society which places a lot of value on the legality of arrangements. When people think of a deal, they think also of an agreement that will stand in a court of law. For almost every decision we make, there is a legal implication.

Every time I download new software on my computer, I am required to click on an acceptance button in order to register my agreement to the provisions set out by the software manufacturer. The truth is that the agreements are so long and the font size so tiny that, to save myself the frustration, I simply click, 'accept'. Whenever I do that a thought tugs at my mind, 'what if the software company has a clause in there that will make them privy to vital personal information on my computer'? Sometimes I would take the time to read the agreement, other times, I simply brush aside the disturbing thought and move on hoping that nothing wrong will happen. What if some mischievous person actually inserted a destructive clause in the agreement? You see, all of us have some Esau tendencies in us. We take too much for granted and trust rather naively that, people are thinking of our best interest when they deal with us.

There could be real danger lurking behind some of the things we take for granted when we sign insurance agreements and financial agreements with our banks and even eat in restaurants. Sometimes in the rewriting of contracts to include new provisions we have agreed to, it is possible for tiny changes to be made on the old provisions.

GOD AND LAW

In the church world where we operate, generally on the principle of trust, people tend to get offended when an agreement ought to be signed legally. We interpret that as a sign of mistrust for one another. I have seen many Christians start a business deal that ends up with so such misunderstanding and acrimony that dishonours the name of the Lord. However, contracts must not be seen as instruments of mistrust but as protective instruments for ourselves and the ideals we have agreed to. Didn't God Himself put His contract into writing? He wrote down all the tiny little details of all the provisions He gave to Israel into a document called the law. The law was signed and sealed with the blood of animals.

SIGNING BINDS YOU

What makes a transaction legitimate is not the terms agreed on, but the signing of the documents. Esau could have made a bad deal, realized it and backed off the deal. He could have said to Jacob, 'Let me seek some advice on this'. He came from a society that did not take the name of the Lord in vain. His society honoured God so much so that they did not even mention his Name. To think that a person from such a God-revering family would swear an oath without much thought, further paints the picture of Esau as a reckless individual. He took so much for granted and hoped that in the end everything was going to turn out right. Much as it is alright to have good intentions, it is very beneficial to back up good intentions with good actions.

> What makes a transaction legitimate is not the terms agreed on, but the signing of the documents.

It is very advisable to seek for expert counsel before you commit yourself to any transaction of significance in your life. I believe in freedom of choice but responsible freedom of choice is exercised after a clear understanding of the implications of the choice. Seek advice before you commit yourself to a boyfriend or a girl friend. Seek counsel before you marry. Seek counsel when there is problem in your marriage. Seek counsel for your business and the moral choices you have to make.

◼ As you negotiate improtant phases of pasage in your life, don't jump into finalities until you have had all the issues well explained to your clear understanding by one who has successfully negotiated such a phase in his or her life.

◼ It is vital that the person you seek counsel from be one who has some good track record in the area you are in.

■ As a very responsible person, you must nurture a network of wise men and women in all the various spheres you function. These are those whose counsel will help you make up your mind.

■ If you don't understand what you are reading, seek advice before you sign. And I don't mean that in only legal matters. Seek specialized advice also from those who know about the technical implications of the subject matter.

When I am buying a property for my church, I will want to talk to a pastor who has successfully bought a property like what I want to buy. In addition to that, I will also talk to real estate and legal experts who have some experience at the level of my operation. In making such a decision I will not, for example, talk to a pastor with a small congregation or a young lawyer who has no experience with the budget I am working with. Esau could just have saved himself a lot of trouble if he had spoken to his father about the deal he was about to sign. A little time off to seek expert advice would have brought the full import of the choice he was about to make to his attention.

ESAU'S ATTITUDE TO CONTRACTS

After Esau had signed the contract with Jacob, he felt he had the better deal because he had food and Jacob had nothing except something in the future called a birthright. Esau felt he had won a better deal for himself because at that point in time, he had something tangible to partake of. He had in his hand food to fill his stomach. Jacob apparently had nothing that he could eat there and then. He had to delay the day of benefit.

Esau walked away from that transaction, and acted as if nothing had taken place. We are talking about a fundamental rearrangement of life here, yet the import was sadly lost on him. He just got up, picked his dinner plate and walked away. He was in a hurry to find a good seat under a shady tree where he could relish his tasty stew and later lick his fingers.

CAN YOU REALLY CROSS THE BRIDGE WHEN YOU GET THERE?

I have seen people, organizations and governments settle for bad deals because those deals did not have immediate consequences. Under intense pressure, they agree to an arrangement that offer temporary relief from a bad situation. Because the consequences are delayed, they walk off without any sense of what they just gave away. When cautioned about the future consequences of their choices, they tend to philosophize on their situation and say things like, 'When we get to that bridge, we will cross it'. What if you get to the river and find out that you sold the bridge with your earlier transaction? There may be no bridge to use to cross the river when you get there; and you could get permanently stranded. Some deals are so involving that they take away from you any options in the future. You don't have to sign a deal today and later mount an angry protest against the consequences of what you yourself had agreed to earlier.

Esau people and nations, who disregard their future inheritance and options, by allowing present pleasure to determine strategic choices, will always have weakened positions at the point of negotiation. They will also serve those who, in spite of the very little they had, end up making good strategic choices with their future in mind. Jacob did not go to the field but with every choice he made, he had the vision of a greater future in mind. It did not bother Jacob to give up his stew if that decision would guarantee him better options and choices in the days ahead.

> You don't have to sign a deal today and later mount an angry protest against the consequences of what you yourself had agreed to earlier.

The value of Jacob's stew at the time it was cooked was not much but it was used to purchase an inheritance worth far more in value. Esau devalued his future. He devalued his future for the price of a bowl of lentil stew whilst Jacob increased the value of his stew for the worth of a worthy inheritance. What value do you place on what you have?

Chapter 7

THE REAL COST OF JACOB'S STEW

*And Jacob gave Esau bread and stew of lentils; then
he ate and drank, arose, and went his way. Thus
Esau despised his birthright.*

Just look at the sequence here. Jacob gives bread and
stew to Esau. Esau eats the bread and stew, got up
from the place of dinning and went away as if nothing had happened. He had made such a monumental
decision and yet he acted as if it is business as usual. The
nonchalance and aloofness of Esau is very unnerving. He
simply moved on with his life as if this was just another
routine of his day. The import of what he had just done
did not register on his conscience. I get the feeling that
Esau was used to getting away with so much in life that
he had acquired a careless arrogance about his choices.

BIRTHRIGHTS AND LIFE CHOICES

Do you know the number of times people sell their birthrights and have no sense of what has taken place? Some leave the place where they sold their birthright and actually think they have had pleasure and a good time. A young girl wants to be a medical doctor. That is her birthright. She dreams of wearing her doctor's garments with a stethoscope hanging around her neck. She sees herself doing her rounds in the hospital ward and bringing hope to patients and their families. Her dreams could probably have been ignited by her need for significance in life or even to change her family's economic circumstances.

> Some leave the place where they sold their birthright and actually think they have had pleasure and a good time.

Then somewhere along her pursuit, a young handsome and seductive boy comes along and throws out words of sweet nothings into her ears with the promise of love and a life of pleasure. Over time, the girl gets taken in by the promise of love and acceptance offered by her young male friend. In the end, the girl negotiates her future, her birthright and destiny for some five minutes of sexual adventure. She probably thinks she has now become an adult and goes home feeling a sense of triumph. For a moment all the dire consequences she was warned about seem far removed from her mind and life. She struts about at school and in the neighbourhood and feels grown up until she wakes up one fine morning with a nauseous feeling. She is pregnant. She considers alleviating the situation with an abortion or offering the baby for adoption. For a lot of girls that is the end of the road for their future. She falls out of school, her dreams of becoming a doctor shatters into little pieces before her eyes as she contemplates the responsibilities resulting from her choices.

The same goes for the young boys. A young man goes to school; he has great expectations. When he is asked 'What are you going to be'? He replies, 'I will be an engineer'. Then somewhere along the line, peer pressure from his friends begins to mount up against him. There is drugs pressure, sex pressure, gang pressure and other pressures to derail his vision. He gets sucked by the drugs pressure and starts to experiment with all sorts of chemical concoctions with the promise of acceptance into a social group. At that moment, he sells his birthright for present pleasure and walks away feeling high and accepted by the friends. Over time, that little experiment with drugs fries his brains and drives him into other excesses that derail his future.

Everyday, a lot of people negotiate away their dreams of greatness and significance for the promise of instant gratification. There are grown married men who sell the peace and joy of their family life to prostitutes. Daily, people are negotiating away who they are going to become for what is available today. *"God is not mocked; whatsoever a man sows that also shall he reap"*. If you sell your birthright today, you will

> Daily, people are negotiating away who they are going to become for what is available today.

not regain your birthright tomorrow. The Esaus of this life are deceived by the pleasures of today. They are deceived by the comfort of today. They are deceived by what they will get today and in that deception, they destroy what they will become in the future.

BIRTHRIGHTS, PROMOTERS AND MANAGERS

Not only do people make moral negotiations that derail their future. They also make business and career choices that are premised on their need for instant gratification. In the world of sports, entertainment and the arts, we read of the stories of the disenchanted. There are all kinds of managers and promoters who do not have a fraction of the talent and skills of the people they manage and yet make a lot of money off the sweat and toil of their clients. How do they do it? They simply look out for a hungry but competent and skillful person from the field. Out there in the harsh world of survival, he finds a young man or woman raised poor, with very little hope for his or her own future, but has very good and potentially marketable skills in a particular field. Those skills are probably used as hobby or in very low key situations. The manager promises the talented person good money for a management contract. They are aware that talented but hungry people are more conscious of their need for immediate relief than they are about who they will become in the future. Hungry people function on short-term survival vision. In this transaction, they provide monetary rewards that are out of the talented person's world.

To the hungry man even junk can sometimes look like food. Hungry people think it is alright to solve today's need and let tomorrow take care of itself. Hungry people have neither time nor the patience to read the words in a contract. What they fail to realize is that tomorrow is only the fruit of seeds sown today. You cannot reap a better tomorrow if you sow a bad seed today. Tomorrow has no power to design itself. It only takes the form and shape of the consequences of our actions or inactions today.

Over time, the hungry fighters become world champions and start earning big purses for their fights. Then reality hits them with the most ferocious knockout punch. They realize that whilst the money they are earning from their fights is impressive, what finally gets to them is pitiful. The decisions of yesterday have become the realities of today. Whilst they had been thinking of their immediate needs yesterday, the promoter had been thinking of their birthright, and their future wealth, and he had made them sell him their future while they were hungry. The case eventually ends up in court where a signed contract is produced. As we are all aware, contracts don't lie. So the promoter smiles all the way to the bank whilst the fighter sweats and bleeds in the ring. This scenario plays out on the soccer pitch, baseball diamond, drama studios and publishing houses. There are young people with great talent who allow their present frustration and pain to define their engagements with managers and promoters. Everywhere that people negotiate contracts and agreements, you are likely to encounter an Esau and Jacob situation.

BE DIGNIFIED ABOUT YOUR HUNGER

If you have to negotiate while you are hungry do not let your hunger show. Keep your hunger to yourself. Be dignified about your hunger; be dignified about your need. Be dignified about your poverty. As a matter of fact if you are going to borrow money, do not appear poor. Appear like somebody who needs extra money not for survival but for increased production. When people sense your vulnerability, they will seek to take advantage of you. Remember your future is always a potential to be revealed and since it is yet to be revealed it may not have much value to you today.

> Remember your future is always a potential to be revealed and since it is yet to be revealed it may not have much value to you today.

Abraham was promised by God that he would be the father of many nations at a time when he was childless. Sometimes your present contradicts your future. Sometimes, who you look like today can contradict who you are going to become. In such situations, it is possible for people to be so concerned with who they are today, that they forget about who they will become in the future.

What you see about yourself today is not the end of your life, so do not act as if this is your last stop. You are in transition, you are moving on to greater things, so be careful about the value you place on yourself today.

For Esau, when the moment of reckoning arrived he found out that, although he seemed to have the advantage of birth and the favour of his father on his side, he was unable to turn the tide of what he set in motion years ago. He worked hard to reclaim his inheritance but the tide of time and consequences were turned against him.

Chapter 8

DON'T GO TOO FAR FOR YOUR GOATS

◇◇◇◇◇

Go now to the flock and bring me from there two
choice kids of the goats, and I will make savoury
food from them for your father, such as he loves.

The moment of the passing on the blessing of the birthright had arrived. Isaac called Esau to him and commissioned him to go in to the field and hunt down an animal. Esau was to use the meat of the animal to prepare a delicious meal for his father Isaac, 'such as my soul loves' and then the birthright would be transferred to him. This was the moment Esau had anticipated all his life – to finally receive the blessing that would ensure a future of greatness for him.

It is not clear from the scriptures if Isaac was aware

of the earlier negotiation and subsequent deal between Esau and Jacob. If he was aware, he probably thought he could over-rule that transaction with his parental authority. If he was not aware of it, then the process he initiated with Esau in order to transfer the birthright to him, was flawed. The reality of the situation was that although Esau represented himself as the de facto first born, he was legally and spiritually not the legitimate firstborn. He had changed his own birth status by a very reckless, nonetheless, legitimate transaction.

Isaac their father, therefore was not in the right when he called Esau and asked him to start the process for receiving the blessing of the birthright. There are parents who sometimes assume that they can rewrite the script for their children after the children have made grievous choices in life. We parents must come to terms with the truth that our children, like every human being, will bear the consequences of their choices. It is hurting to see your children suffer for their wrongs, but when we try to short-circuit the system in order to give them reprieve, we make ourselves partakers of their iniquities. That posture will immobilize us spiritually and make our prayers and decrees of non-effect.

> We parents must come to terms with the truth that our children, like every human being, will bear the consequences of their choices.

As far as the birthright was concerned, Isaac's love and preference for Esau could not overrule the sworn covenant between the brothers. It was a covenant that God respected and honoured.

As Isaac gave instructions to Esau to go way out in the field to hunt down an animal, Rebecca was eavesdropping. She hurried to Jacob to announce that the moment for the transfer of the blessing of the birthright had arrived. It is very obvious that Rebecca was aware of the earlier transaction between the two brothers. She was aware that Esau had sworn and transferred the right of birth to his younger brother Jacob. She knew the implications of covenants that were sealed with an oath. She knew she had to protect the sanctity of the covenant between the two brothers.

Whereas Isaac instructed Esau to go way out into the field for his catch, Rebecca told Jacob to go to the flock of animals reared at home for his catch.

WHERE YOUR TREASURE IS, THERE YOU RUN TO

Esau is sent far away into the bush but Jacob goes to the backyard. Esau's treasure is far away, Jacob's treasure is very close by. As a field hunter, Esau had never developed the technology of harnessing and husbanding his resources in such a way that will save him from having to go to the same place to hunt. Esaus rely on old technology and methods that are time-wasting and ineffective. They develop sentimental attachments to technology for its own sake and not for the sake of its efficiency.

Esaus do the same thing, pursue the same routine and never ask themselves the critical questions that will throw up new alternatives for them. They are always ready to fulfill instructions without suggesting alternatives to the instructor. Esau should have remembered that what his father Isaac was familiar with, might not be the only way to get the job done.

FUFU LOGIC - THE OLD IS BETTER

In Ghana, we have a local staple food called, *fufu*. *Fufu* is made from pounding cooked cassava, plantain, yam or cocoyam together. Sometimes, there is a combination of two or more of these items, which are pounded together. Most Ghanaians will consider themselves not to have eaten until they eat their *fufu* with the accompanying soup. The process of pounding *fufu*, however, is very physically demanding. It takes a lot of muscular power and sweating for about thirty minutes to get a family size *fufu* pounded. We have been pounding *fufu* in this way for probably the last two hundred years or more. Most attempts to simplify the preparation process are met with resistance. *Fufu* connoisseurs believe that *fufu* will not be delicious if any change is made in the old method of preparation. The old method is very unhygienic and cumbersome but people still prefer it. Years ago, a scientist built a mechanized equipment to produce *fufu* faster and in a more hygienic way but that invention was resisted. For most Ghanaians the sound of pounding *fufu* in the evenings has become part of our national identity. This sentimental attachment to the old procedure for making *fufu* has limited the influence of new technology and innovation in this very important area of our lives. I have used the issue of *fufu* here, but in every culture people have tended to allow their sentimentality to slow their access to innovation.

THE ANALOGUE LOGIC

The Swiss have been known and respected for decades as the masters of the mechanical watch. The art and science for fabricating mechanical analogue watches have over the years become part of Swiss culture and synonymous with sturdy Swiss personality. However, the Swiss also invented the quartz movement watch. Although the invention of the battery-operated quartz watch originated from Switzerland, their old paradigm of the mechanical watch caused them to reject the new quartz design. They were so stuck to the mechanical watches that when they themselves invented the quartz watch, which uses electric energy through the battery, they rejected it as "un-Swiss-like."

As a result of that choice, and the fact that they did not expand their watch-making paradigm at that time, their market share in the watch-making industry fell from eighty percent in 1968 to about ten percent today. Their old paradigm prevented them from capturing the future technology of the watch industry. Other nations recognized the new possibilities of the new technology and moved ahead. The Swiss later accepted the reality of the quartz watch as the technology of the future but missed the strategic advantage they would have gained, if they had been more opened to change.

Is your logic digital quartz or analogue? Think about it!

IS THE OLD ALWAYS BETTER?

There are individuals and nations who function from a

productive value system that values sentimental attachments over and above function and benefit. They get so set in the old ways that, even when it is no longer relevant to their present realities, they still stubbornly persist in doing things in the familiar way. They like to do things in the same old way and never have the courage to find faster, more efficient and effective ways of doing what they do. For both the Ghanaians and the Swiss, the comfort and familiarity with what was known, challenged the potential of the future.

The Jacob value system on the other hand, finds ways of saving time and doing what others are doing in a shorter time. They don't hang around old mouldy traditions and practices, which might have had value for a previous generation but have become a hindrance to the forward movement of the present generation.

In my mind's eye, I can picture an anxious and excited Esau, running and sweating in the wild hunting for bush animals. He probably has several near misses as he tried to hunt down at least one animal to fulfill his father's request. Whilst he jumps about and runs after bush animals, Jacob was in the back of the house selecting the best goat amongst the flock. For him, there is no running, jumping or sweating. Just picking out the animal of choice.

Esau is so committed to his hunting that it probably never occurs to him that animals in the bush can be domesticated and bred close by at home. He should have learnt that as much as hunting was a profession he loved, he could start a new business from his hunting that would allow him to breed at home what he hunted in the bush. Many people fall so much in love with what they do that, over time, they lose sight of the reason for doing what they do. The reason Esau hunted was because there was the need for animals which the family could eat and trade for other essentials. Hunting therefore, was a means to an end. Esau got stuck with the means whilst Jacob moved to develop the end.

> Many people fall so much in love with what they do that, over time, they lose sight of the reason for doing what they do.

JACOB INVESTS IN EXPERTS WHO DELIVER

Jacobs prepare good meals because they team up with practicing experts. For this assignment, Jacob teamed up with his mother, Rebecca, who was an expert in preparing for Isaac meals 'such as my soul loves'. Jacob did not have much cooking experience to prepare the special meal his father required so he relied on the experience and expertise of his mother. That reveals one of the traits of those who operate with the Jacob system. They don't try to do it all by themselves when they can receive expert help to save them time, money and anxiety as well as provide them with best quality. It is vital to know the difference between what you can do well by yourself and what you would need a specialist to help you with. Every successful person cultivates a network of experts such as attorneys, financial advisors, stock brokers, insurers, doctors, spiritual counselors and other specialists in the vital areas he operates in for help and guidance. When your tooth hurts, you don't try to pull it out by yourself - you go to the dentist. By the same token, when you don't know how to cook a good stew, you get an expert to do it for you.

Esau was already good at preparing meals that were very satisfying for his father Isaac. As a result, Jacob was disadvantaged in responding to Esau's competition all by himself. Although the birthright had legally changed hands during their earlier transaction, the implementation of the deed was based on Isaac blessing the one who prepared a savoury meal for him. You know, there is a very big difference between what you deserve and what you get. To counter the threat of Esau taking the blessing from him, Jacob had to rely on an expert with more experience than Esau. Jacobs make use of the abundant resources available through others. Sometimes, people take pride in the fact that they do everything by themselves.

YOU DON'T ALWAYS HAVE TO DO IT YOURSELF

When I was a child, my mother used to personally sew all the clothes my siblings and I wore. She would use her old pieces of cloth and other household fabric to sew attires for us. She was able to put clothes on our back although I can not say much for her fashion sense. Some of the 'designer' clothes ended up embarrassing us before our friends. It is the thinking of the 'old school' to sew your own clothes, rear your own chicken, milk your own cow and do your own plumbing. If these are done for recreational purposes, then fine. However, if this is done because we do not want to pay experts with our money, then we need to re-appraise our professional productive philosophies. For domestic use, we could accept the industry and ingenuity of parents who raise their children on meager salaries trying to save up by doing things by themselves. I applaud my mother and many women like her who had to practically raise their families alone. However, that same attitude to do things all by themselves when practiced within a professional work environment could have very negative consequences on productivity. In spite of all the value gained in trying to do everything by ourselves, we invariably end up losing focus on the most crucial areas of our lives where we are real specialists. When their birthright is at stake, Jacobs don't compromise on quality and excellence. They will trust in the best minds to help them solve their problems.

> In spite of all the value gained in trying to do everything by ourselves, we invariably end up losing focus on the most crucial areas of our lives where we are real specialists.

A note of caution. In seeking the help of an expert though, be particular about having a practicing expert. Experts who know what to do don't beat about the bush with experimentation at your expense. There are a thousand and one armchair experts who talk the talk, but have not walked the walk. They may have long degrees but short relevant experience. Such people are not practicing experts of what they profess. They have no track record of past achievements in relation to the area of your pursuit. When you get stuck whilst following their directives, they have no practical references to offer to get you unstuck. Most of the time they will be looking up to you to come up with the answers when you have paid them good money to help you with your assignment.

If you have to pay for expert services, invest your money and time looking for a good hands-on expert like Rebecca who had real life experience in preparing stew, 'such as my soul loves'.

ISAAC CANNOT TELL THE DIFFERENCE

After Rebecca had prepared the meal, it was set before Isaac to eat. He ate it and was not able to tell the difference between a meal prepared from animal meat from the backyard and his own preference for bush meat. Can you believe that? He couldn't tell the difference! The meal he ate although prepared out of meat from the flock in the backyard, still met Isaac's requirement for a meal 'such as my soul loves'. So the trip of Esau was really a waste of time and a diversion. He could have prepared a meal 'such as my soul loves', without necessarily going far out into the field.

We must be careful of the instructions and demands of old Isaacs. An old Isaac is a person, system, or idea which had great success in the past but has failed to update their experience and concepts in the light of new and more efficient practices. They can send you on long errands that produce very little results. There are millions of people in the world today, running wild errands based on flawed instructions from an old blinded Isaac, who is a bit out of sorts with present demands. In any pursuit you undertake, be sure that the one whose errands you are running is abreast with current demands. If you are sent on an errand to build your business on industrial revolution processes in this age of information technology, you will end up with a lot of work and perspiration but with very little relevant results.

The only surprise of Isaac was that the meal was ready earlier than he anticipated. He knew how long Esau took to get his assignments completed and was surprised that such a good meal could be ready in such a short time.

The Jacobs prepare their meals earlier because they plan ahead for future demands. They make use of skills of experts in order to reduce the time required for the completion of assignments. They don't run wild errands in the bush just to satisfy the old traditional methods everybody is familiar with.

ESAU ARRIVES LATE FOR THE FUTURE

Whilst Jacob completes his assignments ahead of time, Esau arrives late for his appointment with destiny. After his long search in the wild, Esau returned home with his catch. He set out to prepare the meal the way his father liked it, and presented it to him.

'Father I have done it, I have worked so hard and so long to fulfill your wishes. Now eat what I have produced for you', he said. That was when he had the most shocking announcement of his life declared to him. His father said to him, *'Your brother came earlier and took the blessing of the birthright'.* There was weeping, pulling of hair and gnashing of teeth, but all that was too late. Time had caught up with Esau's reckless bargaining. The deal he negotiated for, signed and sealed some years ago had been delivered.

I have heard people accuse Jacob of conniving to steal Esau's blessing. We will look at the ethical compromises of Jacob and their implications later. Yes, he told a lie and deceived his father and that ethical compromise must not be tolerated, but let us not forget that Esau was also trying to deceive Isaac. The truth of the matter was that, it was Esau who was conniving to steal Jacob's blessing. By the provisions of their mutual agreement, the birthright passed on to Jacob after Esau took the stew and swore an oath to seal the transfer of his birthright to Jacob. The blessing of the birthright, from then on, rightfully belonged to Jacob. He was legally and before God, the true heir to his father, Isaac's blessing. He did not steal it; he only inherited it. The one who tried to steal the blessing was Esau. He sold it, got paid for it, received a receipt for it and then tried to steal it back when no one was looking.

THE DECEPTION OF JACOB AND ITS IMPLICATIONS

The lie Jacob told to his father and the deceptive attire he put on presents one of the major dangers for those who operate in his paradigm. It shows how people with great vision and foresight as well as great negotiating skills can end up using unethical methods to access their opportunities. Jacob was smart and took advantage of his opportunities in life, but he also yielded to the panic of losing what he had negotiated for. He allowed that panic and the conspiracy of his mother to pressurize him into deception. This ethical dilemma faces a lot of good people.

- What do you do when you seem to be losing something you have worked hard for?

- How do you play the game hard and fair at the same time?

- What methods are ethical and morally acceptable to use?

- Which experts are you ready to work with and which one's do you avoid?

- When your competitor seeks to take advantage of you how do you fight back?

All of these questions lie at the heart of Jacob's actions. He could have used other honest alternatives such as letting his father know about their earlier transaction as the basis to still get the blessing of the birthright. Being a spiritual man who understood the implications of oaths, Isaac would have transferred the birthright to Jacob if the evidence of the earlier negotiation had been presented.

A patient presentation of the facts would have brought him the blessing without all that disguise and lies. This tells us that under intense pressure to get what is due them, a people with a Jacob disposition may compromise their ethical values.

Many people who have a good ground to inherit what they have strived legally for, sometimes end up entangling themselves in very dubious procedures. Where the honest presentation of the facts would have been enough to turn the case in their favour, they allow the panic of losing what they have worked for to push them into corruption and immorality. When pressed to commit an illegality to back up your legitimate claims, remember that:

■ When you start right, you must end right.

■ Truth has inherent power over deception.

■ No force of deception can deny you of what you have legitimately worked for.

■ A patient and persuasive presentation of your case is your greatest weapon.

■ Your illegality can devalue all your previous righteous efforts.

■ Honesty is still the best policy.

We can not fully approve of all the ways of Jacob in this matter, especially the disguise he put on and the lie he told his father about his identity. Those acts were ethically wrong and contrary to the witness we have of him as a man with an upright character. It should be noted that later on when Jacob migrated to live with his uncle Laban, he reaped the fruits of the deceptive seeds he had sown.

Because of the disguise and deception Jacob used, he allowed questions and suspicions to be raised about the legitimacy of his inheritance. He marred what would otherwise have been a very decent transaction.

However, the fact that he disguised himself and lied should not be confused with who the real heir of the birthright was. The birthright was Jacob's to take because he had legitimately acquired it. His rebuke is that he did not close the deal in an upright manner.

YOU GET WHAT YOU NEGOTIATE FOR; NOT WHAT YOU DESERVE

In life, you don't get what you deserve; you get what you negotiate for. There are those who by the facts of their history deserve failure and yet negotiate success for themselves. There are also others, who by birth and history deserve success and yet manage to negotiate failure for themselves.

I have seen children of preachers become wayward. And I have seen children of the wayward become preachers. I have seen children of the rich become poor. And I have seen children of the poor become rich.

I have seen women with no natural children of their own, surrounded with the love and affection of a hundred children. And I have seen women with several children of their own die in loneliness. In life, you will always get what you negotiate for.

- People with the Jacob disposition understand their limitations in life, but do not passively succumb to their limitations.

- They find legitimate means to access all the opportunities that come their way.

- They form alliances with people who have what they don't have.

- They cooperate with and honour those whose services and help they will require.

- They don't use people and disdainfully dispose of them because they realize that life moves in cycles. You may in future need the help of the person you despise today.

The blessing of the first child's birthright was not Jacob's naturally, but he bargained legitimately for it because he valued it. Esau lost it because he had no respect or value for what was naturally his. What he threw away disdainfully, Jacob took hold of reverently.

YOU REAP WHAT YOU SOW

When we make wrong choices in life, we receive the consequences of our choices. It is a spiritual law, '*Whatever a person sows, that he will reap*'.

Esau was being dishonest and disingenuous about what was happening. He knew he had sold his birthright and yet set out to inherit it. He wanted to eat his cake and have it. Well, that's not how God designed it to work. When you eat your cake, it is gone! That is tough but true. It is truth that applies to all areas of life including where we spend eternity. When you live a reckless and wayward life and reject God's offer of salvation, you negotiate for yourself, an eternity of separation from God. There are those who dishonour God and his word whilst alive and yet hope to be accepted by Him when they die. My friend, eternity is too serious to joke with.

NEGOTIATE FOR ETERNITY

If you want to be sure of your eternal destination, you will have to make the decisions and choices for your salvation whilst you are alive and well here on earth.

Somebody once asked me, 'What will you do if you die and realize that there is no heaven or hell and that what you believed about eternity and life after death was wrong?' I said, 'Well, I will lose nothing because I believe my beliefs have helped me lead a fruitful life here on earth'. Then I asked him, 'What if you also died without Christ as your Lord and Saviour and realized after all that there was a heaven and a hell, and that you did not make it to heaven?' He scratched his head and said, 'I don't know'.

You see, wise people set out an insurance policy to cover themselves for any unpredictable eventuality. They cannot predict all the outcomes of life, but they make arrangements for what they cannot foresee. Life is too precious to joke with and eternity is too serious to treat lightly. Don't you think it just makes sense to ensure that when your life on earth is over, you will be covered for any eventuality? Jacobs do not leave their destiny to chance.

> Life is too precious to joke with and eternity is too serious to treat lightly.

If you want Christ to come into your life and have the assurance of salvation for eternity, you can ask God for that right now before you continue with this book. Just ask God in prayer to forgive you of your sins and then ask Christ Jesus to come into your heart and change your life. Ask Him to lead and guide you and also make a commitment to do His will. After you have prayed that prayer, take time to go to church, get a bible to read and begin each day with prayer.

For every step of obedience we take in line with God's will, there is the release of his favour and blessing on our lives. The blessing of God leads to a qualitative improvement in our lives. Let's see how that blessing of the Lord impacts on Jacob's life.

Chapter 9

THE BLESSING OF THE BIRTHRIGHT

And he came near and kissed him; and he smelled the smell of his clothing, and blessed him and said:

"Surely, the smell of my son is like the smell of a field which the LORD has blessed. Therefore may God give you of the dew of heaven, Of the fatness of the earth, and plenty of grain and wine. Let peoples serve you, and nations bow down to you. Be master over your brethren, and let your mother's sons bow down to you.

■ Blessings are the benefits we receive when we position ourselves in line with the path of God's goodness.

■ Blessings are not arbitrary or selective.

■   Blessings are not luck; neither are they good fortune.

They are the fruits of seeds sown; the end product of choices made by individuals. In the Bible, both curses and blessings are consequential to the choices we make concerning our future. Your choices in life will either lead you into a life of blessings where good things happen to you or into a life of curses where everything seems to turn against you. When Isaac blessed Jacob, he was releasing the benefits due him because of his productive response to life and the choices he had made earlier. It would have been wrong for Isaac to have pronounced those same words of blessing on Esau because Esau's life choices up to that time, did not place him in line to receive the benefits of those blessings. Jacob was neither fortunate nor lucky; he was blessed. God promises in His word, *'If you are willing and obedient, You shall eat the good of the land; But if you refuse and rebel, You shall be devoured by the sword"; For the mouth of the LORD has spoken'.* **Isaiah 1:19-20**

CONDITIONS FOR THE BLESSING

Before Isaac blessed Jacob with the four birthright blessings, he smelt the aroma of Jacob and judged it as belonging to a field God has blessed. A field represents the space you operate in. All of us operate in one field or the other to make a living and to contribute to the Divine mandate of managing the earth's resources on

God's behalf. We do not work in the same field, but when you follow the Jacob paradigm and commit to its value system, your field will be blessed no matter what field it is. Certainly it has to be a field whose product honours God and enhances human life. A field whose products and effects devalue human life cannot expect to receive God's approval and favour.

The faithful stewardship of Jacob can be replicated by people across fields as wide-ranging as preaching, marketing, law, medicine, teaching, finance and banking, sports, news media, information technology, agriculture or zoology. Whether you are an employee, self-employed or an employer in your field, the blessing of the Jacob paradigm will give you a new aroma and significance. Jacob went through all these various phases in his life; he was at one time an employee, then he graduated to be self-employed and finally as an employer. In all these phases Jacob was blessed and productive in his field.

SPREAD YOUR AROMA OF SUCCESS

Success has its aroma. Isaac blessed Jacob not only with the blessing of a productive field, but also the aroma that goes with it. When you are blessed it must smell on you. The aroma of a substance is the external expression of its essence. Aromas create atmosphere. When aromas are released, they pervade an atmosphere and control it to suit their character.

> When you are blessed it must smell on you.

During the period of the Old Testament, the Temple of God was always filled with the sweet aroma of curious incense that wafted through the environment of the place of prayer, creating an atmosphere that helped remind the people of God's presence. Any Jew who smelt the aroma of the curious incense became aware and conscious of the presence of God and His power to answer the prayer of His people. If you were depressed, that aroma would renew your strength and reinvigorate you.

Our nose, as a sensory organ, functions as an information gate that helps our brains to determine how to respond to different atmospheres. We judge things by how they smell. When we are around scents that agree with us we stay around to enjoy the aroma. When we are around scents that we don't like, we move away from them. Certain scents provide soothing comfort and warmth whilst others repel us. Newborn babies have their smell. Hospitals have their smell. It is possible to smell life and health in a place. It is also possible to smell death and negativity in a location. Isaac blessed Jacob with the blessing of the aroma of a field the Lord had blessed. Anyone who has visited a farm that has just been rained upon will have an idea of what that smell is like. It is a scent of freshness, newness and life. You feel like embracing the earth or rolling all over the ground.

When people met Jacob, they would sense newness, freshness and life. This was the kind of good feeling that would make people trust him in their business transactions. The blessing of a field blessed by the Lord, made Jacob an attractive person. With this blessing on your life, you will be able to alter the state of all negative atmospheres you operate in. You will literally carry your enabling environment with you wherever you go.

MOVING TO THE NEXT LEVEL OF EXCELLENCE

The blessing of Jacob was a four-fold blessing that opened the doorway for him to have access to a quality of life that would eventually position him in leadership over his older brother. The release of the blessing he received was because of the value system he had operated his life with. This helped him to harness all of his resources to engage in a prudent negotiation for a better life. The birthright blessings took Jacob from phase one of his life into the next level where he would see accelerated growth in wealth and influence.

He had more challenges ahead of him as well as great opportunities to surmount those challenges because, the birthright blessings did not exempt him from the struggles associated with every successful life. The blessings recognised that he had been a faithful steward in little things and was now ready to play in the big leagues and later establish a pattern on which God would build a Nation.

Notice how the scriptures set out the sequence, *"And he came near and kissed him; and he smelled the smell of his clothing, and blessed him and said: Surely, the smell of my son is like the smell of a field which the LORD has blessed. Therefore....."* It was only after Isaac verified the aroma expressed from Jacob's faithfulness that he proceeded to bless him. You move into these blessings when you have on you the aroma of a faithful and successful stewardship of God's resources invested in you. Jacob had passed his level one exam; now it was time to move to the next level where great opportunities and opponents were waiting for him. The four areas covered by the Birthright Inheritance Blessing were:

1.   The blessing of the dew of heaven
2.   The blessing of the fatness of the earth
3.   The blessing of abundance of grain and wine
4.   The blessing of Leadership

Those who function in the paradigm of Jacob and faithfully harness their resources to useful advantage, inherit these four beneficial blessings.

THE BLESSING OF THE DEW OF HEAVEN - DIVINE FAVOUR

The First blessing of the birthright was the blessing of the dew of heaven. Dew is the gentle mist of water that nourishes and moisturizes the earth in the mornings. That is how the earth was watered in the Garden of Eden. It was not a torrent of rain. The falling of the dew is not easily perceived but it efficiently waters the earth. Because of its gentleness, it does not erode portions of the landmass when it falls. That is how Isaac described the first blessing of Jacob. He will receive the blessing of the dew of heaven. This is in reference to the gentle favour of God that provides constant refreshing to us. It is not going to be the rain, but the dew. The dew falls every morning; the rain falls only during certain seasons

There are those who pray for and always expect one big mighty thunderstorm to satisfy the thirst of their land. They spend days and weeks praying for one big mighty miracle to change everything about their lives. Yes, they may receive their one big thunderstorm of miraculous intervention only to realize that, it did not give them all the moisture and nourishing they needed for the rest of the days ahead. The rains are occasional but the dew is fresh every morning. God desires to bless us daily so as to nourish us to face every new day and challenge with fresh energy and wisdom from above. The favour of God's dew will bring you into the ability to use creativity and innovation to produce new wealth from old resources.

> The favour of God's dew will bring you into the ability to use creativity and innovation to produce new wealth from old resources.

THE BLESSING OF THE FATNESS OF THE EARTH

The second blessing of the birthright is related to the fatness of the earth. Fatness refers to richness. To be rich is not the same as to have abundance. Abundance deals with quantity where riches deal with quality. Quality has to do with the excellence and skill that is used to increase the profitableness of a product. The fatness of the earth therefore, refers to the diversity and value that can be derived from the earth. All the properties and products of the earth possess almost infinite productive possibilities for exploration and usage. Different generations have made different uses of the same materials of the earth.

A thousand years ago, people made horse carriages from the earth's resources; today we make shuttle planes and space exploring equipment from those same resources. Just thirty years ago, the main tool for word processing that mankind fabricated from the earth's resources was the manual typewriter; today personal computers with huge capabilities have replaced the manual typewriter.

The earth is so rich with possibilities. Science and technology continues to find new and sometimes more efficient uses for items we are very familiar with. We thought sand was of no value until silicon chips were made out of them. Metals from the earth keep producing new tools and implements to make our lives more comfortable. The blessing of the fatness of the earth, is the ability God gives to us to create new and beneficial products from the earth' resources. Who knows what great leaps in technology still await to be discovered?

It is only when you become a master of creative excellence and quality that you can multiply your products abundantly. To get to that level, more sophisticated production and management skills will be required.

THE BLESSING OF ABUNDANCE OF GRAIN AND WINE

The third inheritance blessing of the birthright that Isaac released into Jacob's life had to do with the abundance of grain and wine. Grain is a primary commodity; Wine is a processed commodity. This blessing has to do with commercial and industrial production of both primary and processed commodities. There are those who produce abundance of items only at the primary level, but have not moved on to the higher competitive levels of productivity. Our capacity to produce large volumes of what we have, whether in the skills of our profession or in the objects we manufacture, is an important key to realizing the blessing of God on our lives. There are nations whose total economic life rests on its capacity to produce one commodity in abundance. If those nations can expand their economic base to include other commodities that can be produced in large volumes, they can experience more ease in their economic life.

GOALS AND SOULS

Let me give you a simple analogy in the field of sports. The soccer player, for example, who scores a large number of goals adds value to his professional career and helps his team win. Some of those sports men and women literally become industries themselves and the basis for a whole new economic empire. At the height of his sporting career, Michael Jordan's skills and presence supported a four billion dollar sales and services industry.

In the field of Christian missions, the evangelist who leads large numbers of souls to Christ expands the kingdom of God. In the retailing business, the company with the largest distribution network and outlets becomes a market leader. The television station with the largest number of viewers increases its market value. The church that reaches out to the largest number of people in its community increases its influence in that community.

When the largest producers of oil have an OPEC meeting, it affects the world's economic temperature! Numbers are important to our growth and blessing. Microsoft captured and controlled the market of computer operating systems because, they made it easy for computer manufacturers to use their Windows program as the uniform operating system. Because of the volume and pervasive usage of its windows operating system, they became the leaders of their industry and had the virtual monopoly to introduce their other software applications as standard tools for computer users.

When Isaac blessed Jacob with the abundance of grain and wine, he was empowering his son into leadership. He was releasing Jacob into a level of massive increase in production such as would make him occupy a leading role in his field of endeavour. Remember that Jacob was primarily, a rearer of livestock. With the blessing of abundance, he had the capacity for increase released into his business. Later when he worked with his shrewd uncle, Laban, Jacob overcome great injustice against his efforts to emerge with a large flock that was far larger than his uncle's.

When our quality is excellent and our distribution is vast, we enlarge our borders and increase our influence. Rarity creates value for discerners; abundance creates value for the multitudes. Some people's success depends on rarity whilst other people's success depends on abundance. In either case, the blessing of the abundance of grain and wine is the blessing that increases your market reach and penetration.

> Rarity creates value for discerners; abundance creates value for the multitudes.

Those who through divine favour, use innovation to create and multiply new products, naturally move into leadership in their field.

THE BLESSING OF LEADERSHIP

The fourth and final blessing of the inheritance that Jacob received placed him into leadership over his peers. This blessing is consequent to the fulfillment of all the previous blessings. Leadership is not forced on people but recognized and appreciated by those who benefit from its influence. Those who impart freshness and newness wherever they are, operate under divine favour. They create diversity and excellent quality out of their enterprises; they produce abundantly out of both primary and processed commodities, and inevitably end up as leaders of people and nations. It is not magical. It is simply methodical. If they worked their way through the process, they became leaders in their fields of endeavour.

There are those who like to throw their weight about ordering people to submit to their authority and leadership. They seek power and influence without meeting the prerequisites for true leadership. They think leadership is the same as bullying and shoving their way into other people's lives.

Jacob's blessing brings him into personal, family, community, national as well as international leadership. He grows in leadership and influence from one degree to the other. True leadership is progressive and dynamic. Anyone who does not have the patience to cultivate his leadership and influence gradually, risks losing the position of advantage he has. Growth allows us to master the various phases of our progress in leadership. Can you imagine what will happen to an individual who becomes an international leader without the anchor of personal or community leadership? He will not have the depth to sustain the heights he has risen to.

Isaac empowered his son Jacob with the ability to move his life from a simple pastoral boy into an international world leader. Jacob grew and eventually had his name changed by God to Israel - father of the nation bearing his name.

Anyone who grows into the fullness of these four blessings of Jacob must be ready to deal with pathological jealousy and envy from other non-performing practitioners in their field.

Chapter 10

ESAUS WITH BAD ATTITUDE

❖❖❖❖❖

So Esau hated Jacob because of the blessing with which his father blessed him, and Esau said in his heart, "The days of mourning for my father are at hand; then I will kill my brother Jacob."

"It's not fair. It's not fair." We hear this complaint over and over again in our world. Employees angrily protest, "It's not fair." Nations argue, "It's not fair." Business owners claim, "It's not fair."

Two cousins were born on the same day and grew up side by side. They learnt everything together. They became devoted friends. Eventually they began to drift apart and develop different likes and interests. One cousin loved books and decided to study hard while the other cousin chose to spend his days playing games and pursuing the less tedious things of life. As fate would have it, the more studious cousin eventually became the adviser for the King while the fun-loving cousin ended up as a deck hand on the royal yacht.

One day, the King and all his advisers set out on a journey up the river. They sat under a beautiful wide canopy and were served with the finest of food and drink. The sight of his cousin seated with the King irked the deck hand immensely. "Here I am working myself to death while my lazy cousin sits at ease with the King", he thought to himself. The more he thought about it the angrier he grew. He got so angry that he started grumbling to the other deck hands about the "lazy advisers".

Later that evening, they docked for the night and went ashore to sleep. In the middle of the night the deckhand woke up when a hand was placed on his shoulder. It was the King. "A strange noise is coming from over there", said the King pointing in the darkness. "Please find out what it is for me."

The deckhand ran off to do the King's bidding, pleased that he was selected for the job. He returned quickly and reported, "It is only a cat which has just birthed a litter of noisy kittens."

"Kittens?" responded the king. "How many are they?"

"I didn't count", replied the deckhand. "I'll go back and check"

Off he ran again to count the kittens and came back. "Six kittens", said the deckhand.

"How many males and how many females?" asked the king.

Once again the deckhand did not know and he had to run to check. "Three males and three females," he panted when he returned. "I see," said the King. "Come with me." Together they went to the lower deck where the deckhand's cousin, who was also the King's adviser, was asleep. The king woke up his adviser and asked him to go check out the strange noise up the hill. When the adviser returned, he had all the details the King could possibly ask about the litter of kitten. He even gave details of the cats' owner who turned out to be the mayor of the village. The mayor had sent his apologies to the King for any disturbances that the kittens caused him. In addition, the mayor also sent a dinner invitation to the king.

At this point the King looked at the deckhand. And said, "This afternoon I overheard you grumbling to the other deckhands about your lot in life. You felt that it was unfair for your cousin to be seated with me and working in such a high position. This little assignment I gave to both of you is a clear demonstration of why you are in different positions in my staff. I had to send you four times for answers. My adviser went just once. That is why he is my adviser and you are working on the decks." There are those who at one try achieve the excellence that others would use four tries to achieve. These are the leaders. Some others also use four times the effort to achieve the excellence of others. They are followers.

> There are those who at one try achieve the excellence that others would use four tries to achieve. These are the leaders.

Yes, sometimes there would be real injustices that need to be corrected in various human situations. The injustices of slavery, apartheid, Nazism and racism for example, are real injustices against certain vulnerable groups. There have been times when people who were better endowed either militarily or financially, have cruelly taken what belongs to the weak forcefully. To use your advantages in life to forcefully take from others is a gross abuse of your skills and resources.

However, there are also Esaus, like the deckhand, who after squandering their opportunities in life realize too late in the day, the consequences of their choices and cry, 'It's not fair'. When Esaus cry, 'It's not fair', they act as if the whole world owes them a living. They conveniently forget the choices they made a while ago, and just focus on their present disadvantage. Esaus like to play the victim and work hard to seek society's sympathy for their cause.

They act recklessly and then after some time, they come face to face with the consequences of their earlier choices and actions. They realize after getting to the river that there is no bridge to use to cross the river. It's too late; they negotiated away their bridges in their moments of desperation. To make matters worse, they realize the river is infested with crocodiles. They find themselves stranded on the riverbanks and then they lift up their eyes and see Jacob on the other side moving on to greater things. The force of their stupidity hits them hard in their own faces and makes them look very dumb and foolish for the choices they made earlier. Everybody who hears the story of their earlier choices, looks at them in a funny way. People gossip about their little intelligence and make nasty comments behind their backs.

That is when Esau begins to contemplate the murder of Jacob. He somehow reasons that, if he can get rid of Jacob, he may regain his birthright and put an end to the endless embarrassment. We must note that getting rid of your competitor does not necessarily make you strong. It is like the story of the short King who eliminated all the tall people in his kingdom only to realize afterwards that he was still short.

Our world is full of angry Esaus who spend much of their lives trying to get at successful Jacobs. When Esaus get angry, they want the whole world to join them in their anger. They sometimes mount incessant campaigns to smear the image of a Jacob or assassinate his character. Any time they see Jacob, they remember their own folly. Behind the mask of many vociferous campaigners, lies a personal frustration with their own lives because of bad choices they made in life.

ESAUS EASILY BECOME DESTRUCTIVE.

An Esau makes a bad choice when he is young in the area of education and drops out of school. At the time he drops out of school, he does not contemplate the consequences of an adult life without education. He exchanges the birthright of a good education for the stew of gangs or drugs and quick money on the streets. For a time, the taste of his stew is very delicious. As he grows he realizes that his options are getting slimmer and slimmer. He discovers that the schoolmates he thought were punks and wimps are making some good progress in life. He later finds a menial job in a company only to find that the CEO was an old classmate. He tries to rebuild familiar ties and finds out that the gap between them is too wide to bridge. What does he do? He probably mounts a very personal attack against the old schoolmate who is now his boss. That is Esau's response when he discovers his own folly. He wants to kill Jacob.

ESAU FATHERS

There are Esau fathers who negotiate away their parental responsibilities for present pleasure. Instead of spending time with their children which is their true birthright, they choose to spend time with their girl friends and have fun. Some spend all their time brooding within themselves and fighting with their wives. Others spend all their time on their work. They do all these only to find out later that, they have lost their children.

> You see, Esaus always feel angry when the consequences of their bad negotiations catch up on them.

When the children grow up and respond more to their mother because she was careful to invest quality time in them, the fathers get jealous and call the mothers names.

When the children become wayward the father blames television, the school system, politicians, bad neighbourhoods or the church.

You see, Esaus always feel angry when the consequences of their bad negotiations catch up on them.

ESAU MOTHERS

Some girls and women want to have irresponsible sex and not think about the children who result from their choices. Women want to have their pleasure and get rid of the defenseless children in their wombs with the argument that it is their own bodies. Well they may have had sex with their own bodies but the children in their wombs are not tumors and growths in their bodies. Those children are lives that need to live. When women make sexual compromises, they must consider that there are consequences affecting birthright involved. It is not all pleasure and satisfying present need. There are consequences to every choice we negotiate for ourselves. Sometimes these same women who showed very little discretion in their personal choices, become very bitter against society and hold it to ransom. They respond angrily to their own indiscretions and blame everybody, but stop short of accepting the responsibility for their earlier choices. Young boys and girls must learn that there are real and painful repercussions to their choices.

THE CAMPAIGN OF ESAU NATIONS

Sometimes, Nations with dictatorial Presidents end up with major economic losses that wreak serious havoc to the standard of living of the citizens. Most so-called third world nations hold within their land mass unimaginable wealth and resources that could obliterate poverty from their countries in a few short years. They have capable and trained human resources who have been persecuted to flee out of their countries. Most of these persecuted citizens end up contributing to the development of other nations. The tragedy of starvation, disease, illiteracy and naked poverty in lots of countries are directly related to governance based on the Esau paradigm. The suffering of the citizens bear the trade mark of dictators and despots who negotiate away the future opportunities of their citizens for some 'stew' in Swiss bank accounts. These leaders are directly responsible for the dehumanizing conditions in their countries. Yet, some of these same leaders attend conferences and make angry speeches against exploitation, imperialism, neo-colonialism and globalization. They hide behind the legitimate concerns and themes of the world's poor and marginalized, to obscure the true facts of their self-gratifying choices that gave away huge chunks of their national treasures to foreign exploiters.

MY 'TOO FAR' REAL ESTATE DEALINGS

Years ago, I had an offer to buy land in a part of our city that was just beginning to develop. The location was considered to be quite a distance from the centre of the city and as such, 'very far'. The price was very good and generous and I had opportunity to purchase several acres. The property on its own was very beautiful but there were not many developments moving into that area of town. I saw the property, liked it but said to the vendor, 'it is too far from town.' I left the property with the 'too far' mentality and decided not to purchase the land. About ten years later, that area became the most prestigious location in the city. Property prices had appreciated highly and only the wealthy could afford to purchase property there.

> The future looks like a new born baby with blood all over it. At the time of birth babies don't look beautiful and cuddly. However, after they have been washed and attired, they smell of freshness.

Any time I heard the value of property in that suburb mentioned in conversation, I felt very foolish. For several years after my decision, I avoided driving into that neighbourhood. I did not want to see my folly. Every happy family resident in that suburb, reminded me of my lack of vision.

I was an Esau in that transaction and I hated it. When people realize their folly, they try to avoid the pictures of their folly. I now have a new attitude towards the 'too far' excuse. The future looks like a new born baby with blood all over it. At the time of birth babies don't look beautiful and cuddly. However, after they have been washed and attired, they smell of freshness.

ESAU'S EXCUSES

Esaus like to make excuses like, 'I did not know it was that serious.' 'I was only joking'. 'He took advantage of me'. 'I did not know what I was getting into'. 'Nobody warned me.' 'Do I have to suffer all my life for this?'

They like to blame everybody but themselves. They find it too hurting to their pride to accept that, they made a very terrible choice when they allowed their present need to obscure their value judgments and choices.

Esaus complain about why some people have so much whilst they have so little. I understand that it can be painful to find yourself at the bottom of the ladder and see people moving up all the time. But trying to kill the Jacobs who made better choices than you will not give you back your birthright. Making excuses and avoiding responsibilities will only limit your options and choices.

There is a better way for Esaus to respond to the reality of their folly.

Chapter 11

WHEN ESAUS BECOME JACOBS

By your sword you shall live, And you shall serve your brother; And it shall come to pass, When you become restless, That you shall break his yoke from your neck."

There are two parts to this prophetic word which appear on face value to be saying the same thing.

■ The first part implies that, for so long as Esau lived to pursue a violent vendetta, he would continue as servant to Jacob.

■ The second part refers to a time when Esau would be able to break the yoke from his neck. That would be the time when Esau becomes restless.

True freedom and equity is not gained through violence, but through a committed and consistent struggle against your own limitations. There are those who think that the only way available for them to have a fair share of the world's treasure is to resort to violence. They feel cheated by the world and so resort to violence as a payback to whoever is supposed to be the cause of their poverty. Violence is not a constructive response to the inequities of society. It only serves to perpetuate the subservient role of the marginalized in society.

> True freedom and equity is not gained through violence but through a committed and consistent struggle against your own limitations.

Our prisons are full of people who thought they could solve the problems of society through angry and explosive outbursts. Young men and women who think society has given them a raw deal, easily get enticed by the drive to even out on society through shooting their way into stores and banks. Invariably, they get caught and end up serving long jail sentences that deny them the little opportunities they took for granted.

Isaac said to Esau, 'if you live by the sword, you will continue to be a servant to your brother, but when you become restless, you will break his control from off your life'.

No individual or groups of people have a patent on a particular Esau or Jacob trait. At various points in our lives, we make choices that are reflective of either trait. There are those who begin life as Jacobs and later become trapped by an instant-grati-fying Esau lifestyle. There are also others who start out on a very self-destructive Esau path, but later experience a U-turn in their lives and start living in a Jacob paradigm.

> No individual or groups of people have a patent on a particular Esau or Jacob trait.

WHEN JACOB BECAME ESAU

In the later lives of our Jacob and Esau, there were occasions when the two switched roles. Jacob got into big trouble when he was about to marry. He saw a very beautiful woman who stole his heart at first sight. He was so smitten with love that, he negotiated his seven-year salary as dowry for the hand of the beautiful Rachael. It is quite clear here that sometimes when the heart is in love, the mind goes crazy and does some pretty wild things. Who would have thought that a wise negotiator as Jacob would allow his feelings and the need for instant gratification to so seize his faculties as to drive him to such ridiculous bargain? After he had used seven years of wages to negotiate for a wife, how was he going to take care of his domestic responsibilities? Obviously, that was not part of the consideration of Jacob. Because of how hard-pressed and desperate he was for Rachael, he was taken advantage of and given the wrong woman on his wedding night. He later rene-gotiated another seven year-salary for Rachael - making it fourteen years in all - to get the cravings of his heart met.

In this negotiation for a wife, Jacob became an Esau. He allowed his present need to cloud his long-term needs.

PARADIGM SHIFT

Thomas Kuhn coined the term "paradigm shift" in his book "The structure of Scientific Revolution" to outline the process of change in scientific thought. The concept refers to the change that new ideas and technologies bring about within a society. The term 'paradigm shift' has now gained a wider reference for both personal and organizational change. It refers to the ability of people to shift their paradigms from one mould to another.

First century stoic philosopher, Epictetus observed that, 'People are not disturbed by things, but by the view they take of them.' The way we see things affects us more than the things themselves. Our current knowledge of the human brain and the functions of the central nervous system have shown that, there is a direct and inseparable relationship between the mind and the body. What the mind conceives, the body gives birth to. What the body gives birth to as its actions, eventually constructs the society. To change what happens in the society therefore, our thoughts, assumptions and beliefs must undergo a structural adjustment in the

> What the body gives birth to as its actions, eventually constructs the society. To change what happens in the society therefore, our thoughts, assumptions and beliefs must undergo a structural adjustment in the way our mind 'sees'.

way our mind 'sees'. Some have said that it is impossible to do that. I say it is very challenging but doable. It requires that we become like children. People learn the norms that become their paradigm so they can unlearn them. Many qualities of human life, such as an infant's craving for milk from the mother's breast are part of our instinctive genetic make up. They are things we do because we were born with them. However, when an adult has a specific craving for a cup of coffee in the morning, he is only responding to a learnt behaviour. Because the adult's desire is a learnt behaviour, it can be unlearnt.

ESAU'S PARADIGM SHIFT

For Esau, the unlearning of old habits and the re-learning of new habits that lead to a more productive lifestyle began after he realized that he had lost the birthright. In that moment of utter pain and disappointment, he made a very important value shift. He cried for a compensatory blessing and demanded for any thing that was left out of his father's blessing treasure house. And Esau said to his father, "*Have you only one blessing, my father? Bless me--me also, O my father!" And Esau lifted up his voice and wept.* **Gen 27: 38**

He was not asking for abundance of blessing, but just one blessing out of all that was his, originally.

■ He learnt to put value on what he had previously taken for granted.

■ He learnt the value of little things.

■ He learnt not to take no for an answer.

■ He learnt to persist till he found something to work with.

■ He learnt that he could start small and grow big.

■ He learnt that what he devalued, others will value.

■ He learnt that bad choices have bad consequences.

These lessons led to a major shift in the paradigm of Esau. They helped to transform his responses to life's opportunities from a reckless waster to a careful nurturer. He did not get back his birthright but became a better steward of the resources that God would later entrust to him.

Earlier he had given up the inheritance of the birthright in exchange for a bowl of food; now he begs and cries for a tiny little bit of what was left over of that birthright. In that moment of shock and desperation, Esau realigned his value system. Esau, the one who took for granted the position of favour he was born into and the promise of a great inheritance, now began to realize the importance and value of little things. He could not do much with all the abundance he had, but was ready to start a new life by using the little he had, to achieve much. In a real sense, Jacob helped Esau to set his priorities right in life. Instead of being a prodigal who wasted the marvelous opportunities he had been born into, he became a wise and prudent manager of the scare resources available to him. His cry for just one blessing was heard and responded to by Isaac.

HE RECEIVED THE BLESSING OF RESTLESSNESS

The blessing of his father was *"And it shall come to pass, When you become restless, That you shall break his yoke from your neck"*

Those prophetic pronouncements do not immediately appear as a blessing. However, within those words of Isaac to Esau were the keys to unlock Esau from the shackles of subservience to his brother Jacob. Isaac prophesied to Esau that the key to his transformation from servant to a free man was for him to be restless. Through restlessness, Esau will gain dominion over his life as well as the subservient role to Jacob.

The restlessness Isaac had in mind was a positive restlessness that was not self-defeatist and self-serving. We must be aware that Satan always seeks to pervert a valuable trait for less than noble pursuits. There are those who are restless in their pursuit of vengeance and malice. Others become restless in pursuing degenerative sexual, unproductive recreation and violent activities. That kind of restless pursuit does not produce freedom but bondage to the basest of human desires.

Positive restlessness drives us to pursue the more excellent way. The apostle Paul put it so well when he

> Positive restlessness drives us to pursue the more excellent way.

said, *"Brethren, I do not count myself to have apprehended; but one thing I do, forgetting those things which are behind and reaching forward to those things which are ahead, I press toward the goal for the prize of the upward call of God in Christ Jesus"*. **Philippians 3:12-15**. This commitment to excellence in our life mission creates the restlessness that drives us to accomplish great tasks for God. Restlessness has led to individuals breaking records and barriers set as the standard for achievement and performance.

WHEN YOU BECOME RESTLESS

Restlessness. Esau was told that his state of subservience to Jacob was reversible. He could break the yoke of Jacob around his neck when he learnt to be restless. The picture I have in my mind's eye is that of a bull that tugs against the yoke on its neck relentlessly until it gains freedom. As the bull paces around its confinement, it lunges forward trying to break free. Its neck will become bloodied but it will keep pulling against its yoke of bondage until it either dies or the yoke is broken. That is how restless people also function. They push and pull until they experience the freedom they are looking for. Passive people do not experience freedom. To gain freedom in any area of our lives requires a persistent tugging against the status quo. Those who are content to only function within the boundaries of man-made limitations, deny themselves the joy of exploring new and noble pursuits. Our world has its fair share of individuals who are imprisoned by mediocre expectations and lifestyles. They accept any and every kind of life situation as their lot in life.

RESTLESSNESS BREAKS THE SPIRIT OF APATHY

There is nothing more damaging to a human being than the spirit of apathy. Apathy occurs when we refuse to be affected by what we experience - when we separate our powers of recognition and enquiry from the experiences we go through. There are people who go through the same negative experiences but never stop to find out why those experiences keep occurring. Sometimes they may question what they are experiencing but will choose the lazy way out, by blaming somebody else. Blaming others is a kind of apathy that removes you from the responsibility of your own life and choices. People who become so used to and comfortable with their negative life conditions cannot change that life. It is necessary to be restless and unhappy with those things that keep you constantly weakened and disadvantaged as you negotiate your options in life.

> It is necessary to be restless and unhappy with those things that keep you constantly weakened and disadvantaged as you negotiate your options in life.

RESTLESSNESS LEADS TO A STRUGGLE

Restlessness leads to a struggle against unacceptable but prevailing factors. In political language, restless people are called, 'agitators' or 'revolutionaries'. They are the one's who through struggle and agitation have fought for the independence and liberation of nations from various forms of political oppression. Restlessness places us in a state of alertness and constant vigilance. When we become aware of the consequences of our choices, we apply our hearts to wisdom in all the important decisions of life. The struggle of the restless, creates a positive passion that energizes his drive for a way out of his bondage and captivity. Without passion, we will be bogged down by discouragement. Every new effort creates excitement but when that new effort travels a distance, it loses its initial energy and becomes boring. But boredom does not mean that the pursuit is over; it simply means that you are now mastering the mechanisms of the new process. This phase of your progress is to keep moving, not with excitement but with passion. That strong inward drive is to see the race well run and finished. It takes passion to be a good revolutionary.

ESAU RESTORED

As a result of this change in paradigm, although Esau lost the blessing of the birthright, he was able to recover the losses from his earlier recklessness. He grew into great wealth and prosperity and also grew into great leadership although not to the same degree of significance as Jacob.

There is evidence from the bible that Esau later recovered from his negative attitude and pursued a more productive life. Years later when he met Jacob he embraced him without bitterness. Because of the earlier threat on his life by Esau, Jacob approached their meeting with a lot of trepidation. However, when they met, Esau was both generous and gracious. He said to Jacob, *"I have enough, my brother; keep what you have for yourself."* **Genesis 33:9**. He had learnt his lessons and recovered from his loses. He was not full of revenge again. He had managed to turn around from a wasteful person to a productive and wealthy man. His change in value system and his restlessness after losing the blessing of the birthright, awakened him to a new way of life.

RESTLESSNESS WILL MAKE YOU QUESTION YOUR PARADIGM

To break from the old Esau paradigm, there has to be a willingness to question the core assumptions that feed and prop it up. That simply means nations and people cannot limit themselves to the native knowledge they have inherited and functioned in, but rather offer themselves the advantages of new knowledge so they can explore new possibilities. The ability to think outside your paradigm is very crucial to shifting that paradigm. I had a conversation recently with one of Africa's young and talented development and management executives. He told me about an interaction he had with the supervisor of his graduate thesis. This executive, then a student in a university outside of our continent had presented a thesis providing answers to Africa's developmental problems. His professor, who was not African read and questioned the assumptions of his analysis. The African student responded that since he was African and was a participant in the experiences of his people, he was better positioned to offer answers to his continent's many developmental problems. The professor then questioned him as to whether he felt being a participant of an experience necessarily qualified an individual to objectively address all the issues related to that experience. The professor proposed that sometimes being a participant of an experience could deny a people of the detachment required to do an effective objective analysis.

CAN THE SICK HEAL THEMSELVES?

Can a sick patient, for example, claim that since he has lived with his painful condition for so long, he is necessarily qualified to offer a cure for his own sickness? We could grant that if the sick person was also a doctor then probably he could offer an informed diagnosis of the sickness. Here again, he could be so close to the sickness that he would lose his professional objectivity. It is for this same reason that doctors are not encouraged to provide service to very close relations.

> To offer real answers, those who are participants of an experience must be able to stand outside of their painful experiences in order to separate the real causes of the ailment from the symptoms they feel and live with.

To offer real answers, those who are participants of

an experience must be able to stand outside of their painful experiences in order to separate the real causes of the ailment from the symptoms they feel and live with. When societies do not experience the improvements they desire in spite of their sincere efforts, it usually is indicative of a lack of recognition of important changes that must take place in that society.

Particularly for those of us who belong to the group of nations designated as 'Third World', it is imperative for our nations to re-examine the models of our developmental paradigms. Some of the old assumptions and practices we have used to set the agenda for our development, stand challenged by new discoveries and technologies. Speed and agility of response is crucial to our survival in a globalized world. As such, any culture and paradigm that sets value on slow deliberative and cumbersome protocols as its model for decision-making will find itself constantly out-run and out-paced in the new economy. The crucial challenge is whether we can muster the courage to ask the right questions and to honestly seek for the answers.

WHAT QUESTIONS ARE YOU ASKING?

The quality of your questions will determine the quality of the answers you receive. If you ask the question, 'Why did they do this to me?' you make other people the focus of your examination. You remove yourself from responsibility and let others bear the burden for what you are going through. Those who ask such self-preserving questions;

■ Cannot identify the weaknesses inherent in their paradigm.

■ Cannot identify the weaknesses in their own choices.

■ Confer the power of their destinies on others.

■ Make themselves incapable of changing their own lives.

The other and more useful question to ask is, 'Why and how did I allow this to happen?' Those who ask such questions signal that they are mature and ready to take personal responsibility for their lives. Those who ask such questions are ready for transformation.

■ They signal a readiness to change their paradigm

■ They show that they are ready to alter their changes

■ They empower themselves to shape their destinies

■ They open themselves to other useful options

Those who seek to change their present unacceptable circumstances, must muster the courage to question those attitudes of theirs which have fed the situations they dislike.

THE QUESTIONING MIND

In some societies, the enquiring mind of the child is labelled pompous and disrespectful. The bold, coura-geous and independent-child is stub-born and arrogant. On the flip-side, the tame, docile, timid and unques-tioning child is accepted as good and well-behaved. In such traditional societies, value is placed on certain precise protocols in speech and action, with very little room left for questioners. Children learn from questioning. Sometimes their simple questions can be very irritating; other times very provocative and sacrilegious. They don't question because they desire to start a new revolu-tion but because they have a lot to learn and do not assume that things must just happen. Children know that things don't just happen; they are made to happen. Life is not random; life was created. There is a deliberate cause for our existence and reality. When we understand the cause we will understand the effect. At the heart of enquiry is the desire to know more, remove inconsisten-cies and to affirm truth. When my child asks me a

> Those who seek to change their present unaccept-able circumstances, must muster the courage to question those attitudes of theirs which have fed the situations they dislike.

simple question like 'daddy do you love me?' that child is seeking to find out more about my love, remove any nagging doubts from his mind about my priorities and to affirm truth. Those simple questions from children can change their parent's priorities. I have gone to bed many times reflecting on the innocent, sincere questions of my children. They have ranged from questions like, 'is God air?' to the dreaded 'where do babies come from?' I have standard answers for some of those questions but many times I set to do serious thinking, prayer and re-examination as I look at some of those basic questions again.

RESTLESSNESS WILL MAKE YOU A REVOLUTIONARY

People who raise questions are, often times, seen simply as those who have no regard for order and derive sadistic pleasure from upsetting everybody. Some questioners may fit that profile but the majority of questioners do not have revolutions in mind. It is the result of their questions that create the revolution. A lot of revolutionaries would have shied away from the process they began if they had foreseen the consequences of their ideas. Sometimes they themselves become victims of their own discoveries.

A restless person does not start out with the premeditated notion to generate a revolutionary idea. They start out with the curious honesty of a child to discover. When a little child gets a toy he plays with it for a while and then starts dismantling it to find out how it works. Many children have received some good spanking from adults who spend a chunk of their hard earned salaries to buy those expensive toys. Adults only open the toy when it breaks down. And even that they still will want an expert to do it for them. The child does not wait till the toy stops working in order to discover how the toy works. He opens it whilst it is still working. That is how children express their restlessness. It is not naughtiness; it is just a desire to know. Remember the words of Jesus, '*Assuredly, I say to you, unless you are converted and become as little children, you will by no means enter the kingdom of heaven*'. **Matthew 18:3**. We can gradually create the foundations for a new paradigm to regulate our lives.

A NEW CREATION

Every man or woman who has undergone a genuine "born-again" experience will understand what a paradigm shift is all about. For such a person who encounters spiritual renewal, a radical change in nature, thought and perception occurs that results in very profound changes in life. Alcoholics receive power to be sober; violent criminals become compassionate citizens; promiscuous individuals receive the power of self-control. The words of the old Christian chorus that celebrates the transformation of life says "*the things I used to do I do them no more.*" When we experience a paradigm shift as a group we should also be able to say and sing *"the things we used to do we do them no more."*

These inspired words from the Apostle Paul explain the Christian understanding of a paradigm shift *"Therefore if any man be in Christ, he is a new creature: old things are passed away; behold, all things are become new."*

2 Corinthians 5:17. This 'new creation' experience that the Apostle alludes to, is not limited to our spiritual realities only but, like leaven, it can influence every other area of engagement and raise us from the confines of an old life into the promise of a new reality. People who have received spiritual regeneration have some-times been content to contain that awesome transformational experience only within their spiritual life and have not expanded its possibilities to their social, mental and emotional realities. When people experience a paradigm shift in any area of their lives, the old things pass away and all things become new.

> When we experience a paradigm shift as a group we should also be able to say and sing "the things we used to do we do them no more."

BE TRANSFORMED

And do not be conformed to this world, but be transformed by the renewing of your mind, that you may prove what is that good and acceptable and perfect will of God.
Romans 12:2

Becoming a new person is the beginning of a whole life process of developing a new set of values and a new mould of thinking about your life. The mind will function with the information and exposure we give to it. When we identify the new values we want to acquire, we have to painstakingly learn them.

- Identify those whose lives model the patterns you hope to build your life around and make them your role models and mentors.

- Identify the environments that nurture the paradigms you desire to live your lives by, and expose our minds to them.

- Look out for books that advocate for the paradigm you want to position your life in and read them.

- Build a new network of friend and acquaintances who live their lives around your new core values.

- Constantly monitor your progress in the new direction you have chosen.

- When you fall short of your new expectations quickly make amends and get back on track.

- Build a meditative life of prayer that seeks God's wisdom and guidance for all the choices you make.

In the end, the Jacob way of uprightness, nurturing of resources and forward-looking innovative thinking wins.

"But on Mount Zion there shall be deliverance, And there shall be holiness;

The house of Jacob shall possess their possessions.

The house of Jacob shall be a fire, And the house of Joseph a flame;

But the house of Esau shall be stubble; They shall kindle them and devour them,

And no survivor shall remain of the house of Esau," For the LORD has spoken. **Obadiah 17-18**